Peter Grist

DAYTONA

R/T

DODGE DYNAMITE!

50 Years of Dodge Muscle Cars

VELOCE

CONTENTS

Bonneville record breaker, 1956. Covering 31,224 miles in a continuous fourteen-days-and-nights run, this 1956 Dodge sedan swept to 307 endurance and performance records on the Bonneville salt flats in Utah. Dodge Chief Test Driver, Danny Eames, alternated at the wheel with two others in the record run, which was supervised by officials from the AAA Contest Board. After Bonneville, Eames took the car on a 4000 mile tour of Texas without incident.

BIBLIOGRAPHY AND ACKNOWLEDGEMENTS

ACKNOWLEDGEMENTS

I would like to thank the following people and organizations, who without their help, support and generosity this book would have been impossible to complete and who allowed me use of their photos (photo copyrights in brackets):

Trevor Creed – DaimlerChrysler, Barry Dressel – Walter P Chrysler Museum, Philippe Léost – Point Virgule (book layout), Al 'The Lawman' Eckstrand (photos of his car), Geoff Stunkard – self confessed drag strip nut (historical photos of drag strip cars), Dennis & Karen Kennedy for sharing my feelings on the '56 D-500 (archive pictures of '56 D-500), Simon Elliot – ChryslerJeep UK Ltd (Viper world record photos and press images post 2005), Art Ponder and the Chrysler Historical Dept USA (all archive Dodge press shots pre 2005). Don 'Big Daddy' Garlits (for pictures of his cars), Peter Robain – No.1 Photographer (Viper and Justin Bell photos), Brian Wallace & Scott Sebastian at Dodge Motorsport Division (post 1995 Motorsport pictures), Robert Palmer – Dodge Brothers Club, Hugh Chamberlain Motorsport (Chamberlain Viper), Buzz McKim and Daytona Speedway Museum (archive racing footage from 1952 to 1964), Tim Dupont – Keeper of the last D-500-1 (photos of his D-500-1), Chick Shafer – Ford Talladega (photos of his Talladega and 1992 Daytona Trans-am), Ford Archive Dept UK (for Henry Ford and 1904 model C), Gary Schneider – General Lee (photos of the General Lee), Steven Juliano – The Diamante (www.StevenJuliano. com), and last but by no means least, I would like to thank my wife, Catherine, who kept me sane throughout the compiling of this book.

All other photos taken by the author or taken from author's personal collection along with other adverts, cutaway pictures and diagrams.

BIBLIOGRAPHY

There are many good books on the subject of Chrysler, Dodge and muscle cars. Those listed are only a small proportion, but are recommended as follow-up reading and were of great help in writing this book.

Hyde, Charles K, *Riding The Roller Coaster*, Wayne State University Press, 2003

Craft, John, *Chrysler, Plymouth & Dodge Stock Cars*, Motorbooks International, 1997

Flammang, James M, *The Chrysler Chronicles*, Publications International Ltd, 1994

Girdler, Allan, *Stock Car Racers*, Motorbooks International, 1988

Langworth, Richard M, *Illustrated Dodge Buyers Guide*, Motorbooks International, 1995

Lee, John, *Standard Catalogue of Chrysler*, Motorbooks International, 1990

McPherson, Thomas A, *The Dodge Story*, Crestline, 1992

Mueller, Mike, *Chrysler Muscle Cars*, Motorbooks International, 1993

Sessler, Peter, *Illustrated Dodge & Plymouth Muscle Car Buyers Guide*, Motorbooks International, 1995

My obsession with American cars began some time in the 1960s growing up in England, when I saw a pink and white Chevy Impala, the one with the gull wing fins. What a vision – like something from another planet. I was biking back from school and followed the car through our town as far as I could still headed for home. That was it – I was hooked. I bought *Car Craft*, *Hot Rod*, *Motor Trend*, any and every magazine on American cars I could get.

I bought plastic car kits: AMT, Johann, Revell, and always American cars, custom cars or street rods. I built a 1955 Chrysler New Yorker, a 1961 Imperial and the Chrysler Turbine car.

In 1966, I went on an automotive pilgrimage to a place called Santa Pod Raceway in Bedfordshire, England, where I saw a spectacular Hemi-powered Dodge Charger do a burnout on the drag strip. That car was driven by a Chrysler Corporate lawyer named Al Eckstrand, who toured US military bases in Europe giving demos of his car as part of the American Commando Drag Team. I remember walking all around it, peering into the interior and under the hood, being blown away by the sound of its staccato idle. I never thought I would ever see that car again. That car is now in our Walter P Chrysler Museum Collection, here in Auburn Hills, Michigan, part of our Chrysler Headquarters complex. Santa Pod Drag Racing Association was started by a guy called Clive Skilton, who happens now to be a Chrysler Jeep dealer in California and whom I had the pleasure of meeting in person several years ago.

I still remember seeing and falling in love with the new 1970 Dodge Challenger at the Earls Court Motor Show. It was bright orange. I wanted one like crazy, so is it any wonder that I took the greatest pleasure in being able to oversee the rebirth of the Challenger as a concept car for the 2006 Detroit Auto Show? Who knows, perhaps I will finally get to have one in my garage after all these years.

As the saying goes, it's a small world, isn't it?

Trevor Creed
Senior Vice President, Design
Chrysler

Trevor M Creed was born on 23 September 1945, in Wolverhampton, England. He studied in Birmingham at the University of West Midlands, where he achieved a BFA in Product Design Engineering before going on to work as a designer for Ford of Britain. He stayed in England with Ford until he moved to its North American operation as design director in 1982. In 1985, Trevor moved to Chrysler, initially as Director of Interior Design & Color & Trim. He was appointed Senior Vice President – Design for the Chrysler Group on 1 July 2000. Prior to this position, he was Vice President – Large Car, Small Car & Minivan Design, Chrysler Group. In his current position, Trevor is responsible for directing all activities of the Product Design Office.

Dynamite! This advert from 1957 says it all about the optional D-500 package that became available to all Dodge passenger vehicles.

Since the beginning of recorded time, man has had a thirst for speed. Amongst the leaders in American performance history is the name DODGE, the division of the Chrysler Corporation, now DaimlerChrysler, that from the late fifties to the early seventies fed America's love of speed and power and helped to quench that thirst. For the first time, powerful new Dodge cars are easily available to the UK and the rest of Europe, so now – fifty years on from the introduction of its first performance car, the 1956 D-500 – is a great time to celebrate Dodge muscle cars.

I first became aware of these cars when an Army buddy of mine bought a 1949 Dodge. With a long Cadillac-looking nose and high rear end, it resembled a hearse and did nothing for me. Next to my sporty 1955 Buick Century it looked like a house brick. Having said that, it was an incredibly solid automobile built for reliability and functionality, not style. I bought my first Mopar car, a 1959 DeSoto, a few years later. I did know that DeSoto was American, but that was about it. On further investigation I came to learn that this was yet another division of Chrysler. Hard to believe that the same company could make such startlingly different cars within

just ten years of each other. A house brick on wheels in '49 to the long, low and sleek '59 models.

More research showed no club in England that catered particularly for my car, so I went about setting one up. This was when I found out just how popular Dodges are. Although that club catered for all marques within the Corporation, Dodge owners consistently made over a third of total members. Over the past decade, my wife Catherine and I have owned a 1983 Dodge K-car, a 1987 Shelby Charger (that was ludicrously fast), and currently a 1967 Coronet 440, two Neons (one of them being an R/T) and a 1995 Grand Caravan as the family mover. But I still have a yearning for something with a little more power. A 1956 D500 would be a good place to start, or perhaps a 1969 Charger, and who could resist the mighty Viper GTS-R? So many great cars. One day, yep, one day.

I have written this book with the intention of trying to get across the excitement of these great cars – the history of the developments and successes that they achieved. I have included a brief potted history of where the Dodge name came from, and how it came to be part of DaimlerChrysler.

When reading books on performance cars, especially from Chrysler, the same few cars crop up repeatedly. Daytonas and Challengers spring to mind. They are here too. But, unlike other books I have read, I have tried to include all of Dodge's great performers, from the early fifties with the D-500, right up to the present day with the Viper, racing Neons and the latest Charger. Many of these cars were born from design ideas that came from experimental or concept cars, some of which you will find here as well, along with stars from TV and the silver screen. And a book on Dodge performance cars would not be complete without the actual race cars. Champions from the track and drag strip, in either Dodge or Dodge-powered vehicles, are shown doing what they do best – going faster than the competition. All of this together, I hope, will give you an all-round picture of Dodge, its beginnings, its evolution and its successes, that you might be inspired to read more about these fantastic cars, or go and see them in action (which is still possible), or even better, go buy one.

Enjoy the book.

1

The Dodge brothers, John and Horace, learned their machining skills at their fathers machine shop in Niles, Michigan. In 1899, when John was 35 and Horace was 31, they moved to Windsor, Ontario where they worked together at the Canadian Typothetac Company. It wasn't take long before they started leasing some of this company's facilities to produce a bicycle, called the Evans & Dodge.

The Dodge Brothers badge adorned the radiators of all Dodge cars from their inception in 1914. Over 22,000 applications to become a Dodge outlet were received from prospective dealers, and this before Dodge had even built its first car. The two intertwined triangles signified the brothers' partnership and had no religious significance. The badge would remain unchanged until 1938, ten years after Chrysler purchased the company.

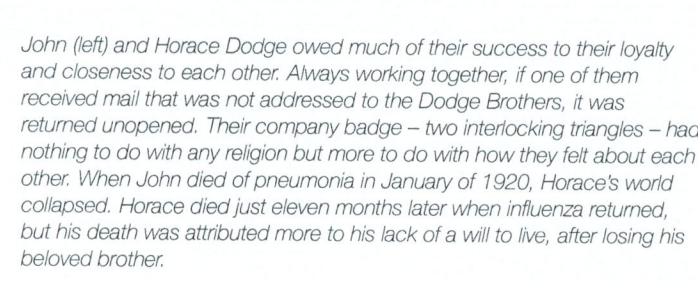

John (left) and Horace Dodge owed much of their success to their loyalty and closeness to each other. Always working together, if one of them received mail that was not addressed to the Dodge Brothers, it was returned unopened. Their company badge – two interlocking triangles – had nothing to do with any religion but more to do with how they felt about each other. When John died of pneumonia in January of 1920, Horace's world collapsed. Horace died just eleven months later when influenza returned, but his death was attributed more to his lack of a will to live, after losing his beloved brother.

By the turn of the century, the brothers had started manufacturing small automotive components for other fledgling car makers, alongside their patented 'ball bearing bicycle'. Success followed, and by 1901 they had decided to return to Michigan to set up their own, larger company. They set up shop on Beaubien Street, in Detroit – the town that was already starting to turn in to 'Motor City'. They soon moved on to larger components including 3000 complete transmissions for R E Olds' new Oldsmobile. By 1903, the cycle was dropped completely as more automotive work took precedence. Their reputation for craftsmanship was already well forged and they quickly established themselves as the largest automotive parts supplier in the world at that time, building on the name for quality and craftsmanship.

Around this period, a close link was forged between the Dodge brothers and Henry Ford. The brothers bought a 10 per cent interest in the new Ford Motor Company and of course supplied many parts and assemblies, including axles and transmissions, and even redesigned many early Ford components. So Ford's Model C took to the road with Dodge-built engines and other key assemblies.

As Ford prospered, so did Horace and John. But by 1914 the brothers, who were now on the Board at Ford, had become disillusioned with Henry Ford's work ethics, so on 17 July 1914 they launched their own company, Dodge Brothers, Inc. With the intention of building their own cars, they set about designing the first Dodge. This news swept the auto industry like wildfire. It is said that over 22,000 firms applied for a Dodge Brothers dealership, and this before the first car had been built!

Just 4 months later, and to much acclaim, the very first Dodge motor car rolled out of the brothers production plant. The date was 14 November 1914. When asked why they had set up in the car manufacturing business, John Dodge replied, "Just think of all the Ford owners who will someday want an automobile."

The first Dodge, the 1914 Dodge prototype. While their legal wrangles with Henry Ford continued, John and Horace carried on with their plans to begin building their own car. Vehicles were designed and tested at the Dodge's huge Hamtramck plant. The first Dodge automobile is seen here parked outside the John Dodge Estate, at 33 East Boston Boulevard, Detroit, on 14 November 1914. In the rear sit the brothers, Horace (left) and John. This prototype had louvered front panels on the engine covers but these never appeared on production models.

These first Dodges were all black 4-door (the driver's was non-opening) touring cars that were very basic in design compared to their contemporaries. A rugged 4-cylinder, 35bhp engine powered a sliding gear type 3-speed transmission. The body was made by Budd, and the vehicle was the first ever American mass-produced, all steel-bodied car. They were, however, quite spartan and devoid of most accessories, though did come with leather seats, reclining canopy, electric lighting, electric self-starter, speedo, windshield and de-mountable wheel rims. Most importantly, they came with the Dodge name for quality and dependability, and were priced to sell at a very competitive $785. Official sources quote that the brothers managed to produce 370 vehicles before the year drew to a close.

The following year saw a sister for the tourer join the Dodge line-up, in the form of a 2-door roadster. Production continued to climb, and by the end of 1915 the Dodge plant had made an incredible 45,033 cars and employed 7000

Dodge test track, 1917. This photograph demonstrates clearly how important reliability was to the Dodge brothers. The test track was part of Dodge's massive Hamtramck factory. The plant was built in 1910 in the Hamtramck suburb of Detroit on Henry Ford's recommendation and covered over 24 acres of land. Notice that all of the cars here have yet to be fitted with headlights. Particularly interesting is the rare center-door sedan shown in the middle ground with a white cover over the hood. These vehicles had a very limited market so were scarce in their day. The cars windows could be lowered and came with wire wheels as standard.

workers. As the first 1914 cars were classed as 1915 models, this total held the record for best first year production thus far in US automotive history. Never had an automobile brand or a new model achieved such success so quickly.

By 1916, Dodge held the number 4 position in the industry after Ford, Buick and Willys-Overland, with more than 70,000 cars leaving the factory. The Dodge Brothers' reputation for dependability, strength and performance grew quickly. Doctors, farmers and delivery companies all made use of the rugged strength of Dodges, getting to locations and people that were not previously accessible by anything other than horse and cart. The military recognized this and began a close relationship with Dodge that continues to this day.

1916 military Dodge. The Dodge name for ruggedness and dependability soon became known to the military, and by 1916 the vehicles were in regular use with the armed forces. This is one of 250 Dodge Tourers that saw service in the Mexican border campaign, and is purported to be the car that a young Lieutenant George S Patton used to lead the first ever mechanized cavalry charge in American history against Pancho Villa. This vehicle also went on to see action in the First World War; it was used to transport General Pershing across Europe. The driver was none other than Sergeant Eddie Rickenbacker, pilot and racing driver. This was the start of a close relationship between the US military and Dodge that continues to this day.

First World War ambulance. Its vehicles were already proven to be very reliable and strong, and Dodge was asked to produce an ambulance for war service. Many differing chassis were used but the design remained mostly unchanged throughout the period of production. This use of Dodge technology was only the tip of the iceberg: almost all American coachbuilders came up with some variant on this theme. Hearses, delivery trucks, semi-trailers, pick-ups, even small buses were built around the early Dodge. This, of course, set the course for Dodge's other well-known vehicles – its trucks.

That same year, General Pershing used a Dodge to chase Pancho Villa across Mexico. At this period in time of course, the Great War raged on in Europe and it was Dodge, more than any other single manufacturer, that shipped its vehicles overseas to the war zone. It adapted the car design into a light commercial vehicle. This first design came in the form of an ambulance and saw service (along with other versions) with the Allied Expeditionary Forces (AEF) from 1917 on.

Following the Armistice in 1918, Horace and John added yet another model to their growing line-up when they debuted an all-steel sedan. In terms of design, Dodges had changed very little since the first cars. Most of the changes were mechanical improvements. The same 4-cylinder engine was still in use and the cars continued to sell. However, tragedy struck in 1920. Both brothers were renowned for their hard drinking and while Horace and John were staying

It is clear from this 1918 four-door tourer that very little changed on the cars in the early years. New models were released but the basic design remained the same. Rather stark and utilitarian in looks, the car came with very few accessories or luxuries. For the base price of $785 a buyer in 1914 got leather seats, electric starter and lighting, a folding top, speedometer, windshield and demountable wheel rims. A small list of optional extras included a horn, side curtains, spare tire, toolkit, running board, luggage rack, wind wings, motometer, a spotlight and wire wheels. But most importantly, the customer got the Dodge name for dependability built in for free. The cars were a great success. The first were powered by a 35bhp 4-cylinder engine that was matched to an unusual three-speed sliding gear transmission. This first engine proved almost indestructible and went virtually unchanged until 1928 when Chrysler introduced a Dodge-Six.

1924 Roadster. From very early on, the two brothers were aware that mechanical reliability alone would not keep the Dodge company alive. Although not style-setters themselves, Dodge vehicles usually looked as good as, if not better than, their rivals. The 1921 four-door open Tourer and the sporty 1924 Roadster were both elegant, stylish and very affordable.

at a hotel in New York City for the National Automobile Show, Horace contracted the flu. This soon became pneumonia. John stayed by his side, willing him to fight the virus.

Horace recovered, only for John to succumb. It is rumoured that weakened by the years of drink, John was not strong enough to fight the infection and died in the adjoining room to Horace on 14 January, 1920. Grieved and weakened by the loss of his very close brother, Horace finally died from yet another bout of influenza some 11 months later in Palm Beach, Florida, on December 10, 1920.

Today it seems hard to imagine how the relatively young and fit could die from flu, but at the time this illness accounted for more loss of life than all the battlefields of World War I.

The brothers, however, did leave the company in a very strong position. Dodge held the number 2 spot at the end of 1920, second only to Ford. Their widows empowered a long time Dodge employee, Frederick Haynes, to run the company. This he did, keeping true to the deceased brothers' wishes and traditions. As time passed profits and production began to fall, due in part to the fact that the Dodge had barely changed in style or mechanics since those first 1914 tourers. In 1921 Dodge had dropped back to 3rd position, and by 1925 was in 5th place. The widows decided to sell. On April 30 1925, the banking group of Dillon, Read & Co paid a massive $146,000,000 – the largest cash transaction ever made at that time.

Of course, these banking men were not car manufacturers, nor did they try to pretend otherwise. They installed one E J Wilmer as head of the company, and under his supervision, the company started a return to sales success. By 1928, the Dodge Brothers Inc was a going concern and, once again, up for sale.

The New Victory Coupe

1928 Dodge Victory Six. When Chrysler finally purchased Dodge Brothers Inc in 1928, the new models for that year had already been released. Falling sales had pushed Dodge towards making a more powerful and modern-looking car. The biggest change was the engine. The same old reliable 4-cylinder engine that had been used in all Dodge cars since 1914 now gave way to a new, sprightly 6-cylinder – the first six in Dodge's history. This new engine gave between 58 and 67bhp, depending on the model purchased. A complete re-style of the bodywork heralded three new series: the base Standard Six, the medium-priced Victory Six and more luxurious Senior Six. This is an artist's impression of the Victory Six rumble seat coupé, a four-passenger hardtop that was arguably one of the most handsome models of that year. The picture was used to advertise the new car in sales literature and the press. However, due to production difficulties, it was never built.

1932 Dodge. The famous Dodge 'Ram' trademark was introduced this year in the guise of a chrome radiator cap ornament. Designed in 1930 by Professor Avard Fairbanks of the University of Michigan, the Ram (undergoing many stylistic changes) would be seen on all Dodge cars up to 1954 (the Ram symbol is still used on Dodge vehicles today, although only as a plastic badge). The car shown here is a Series DL four-door five-passenger sedan. In 1932, 16,901 were built and the car proved to be Dodge's best-seller for that year. The total for all the DL models was 21,042. Total Dodge production was up from 1931's low of 47,300 to approximately 50,100. Although this series used a 6-cylinder 217.8in^3, its larger brother, the DK Series, now had a 282.1in^3 in-line eight. These powerful straight-eights were introduced in January 1930. Although they appeared in one of the worst years of the Great Depression, the cars were still a success, keeping Dodge in seventh place in the industry throughout those lean years.

DODGE DIVISION – 'FLY EATS ELEPHANT'

Walter Percy Chrysler had been making cars under his own name since 1924 and, like the Dodge brothers, had wanted to take on the might of Ford (and later, General Motors), in producing a quality car for the masses. Chrysler's branded cars were, however, very upmarket, and he wanted to expand his empire so that he could offer a car right across the sales spectrum, from low-priced through to luxury vehicles and every stop in-between. He had approached Dillon, Read & Co previously, in an effort to obtain Dodge and its huge production plants, forges and distribution network. They declined his offer. So instead, Chrysler put in to action his alternative plan, and created two brand new car marques. Plymouth and DeSoto.

At the outset, Plymouth became the low-priced economy line, with DeSoto occupying the medium

GREAT WORK, BOYS.... YOU'VE BUILT THE CAR THAT MILLIONS CAN AFFORD TO OWN ! WE HAVE NOW PUT DODGE IN A DOMINANT PLACE IN THE VOLUME MARKET.

*Mr. Chrysler congratulating
Fred M. Zeder and K. T. Keller*

Although America was still in the grip of the Depression, 1933 was a banner year for Dodge. Walter Chrysler's dream team of design engineers comprised Fred M Zeder (former head of engineering at Studebaker), Carl Breer and Owen R Skelton. Chrysler had first used the talents of these 'Three Musketeers' in the early '20s when, after taking up the reins at Maxwell, Walter asked Zeder to come up with a new car to bear the Chrysler name. This winning team stayed with Chrysler and was responsible for just about all the engineering feats achieved by the company throughout the '30s. This well-staged publicity shot shows Walter Chrysler (middle), congratulating Fred Zeder (left) and K T Keller (still head of Dodge Division) on a job well done. And it certainly was. The '33s were all new. A gracefully smoother body was topped off with a fresh, attractively curved radiator, all of which sat on a hand-built chassis. The early DP Series Dodges utilized a 111¼in wheelbase, but on 5 April 1933 a longer 115in wheelbase was introduced which only helped accentuate the new rakish lines of the car. Engineering still ruled, though: a new state-of-the-art L-head six was introduced which gave 75bhp at 201.3in³. This was matched to a quieter transmission that had silent helical gears, another engineering first for Dodge. All of this was enough to boost Dodge to fourth place in the league of auto manufacturers.

sector, and the Chrysler marque, along with its Imperial models, tackling the upper and luxury markets respectively. However, Walter P hadn't given up completely on getting hold of the Dodge name, and was said to be very determined to see Dodge become a Chrysler division.

Fresh attempts were made to buy Dodge and on the 31 July 1928 a deal was struck in a move that saw one company, Chrysler, take over another company five times larger than itself. Media critics at the time described the takeover as 'Fly Eats Elephant', with warnings of failure as Walter P bites off far more than he can chew. No money changed hands, but a stock exchange merger took place that amounted to a cost of $170 million, giving Walter Chrysler complete control. Walter was incredibly keen to get started with Dodge. So much so that when Clarence Dillon phoned Walter the day after the sale, informing him that the Dodge factory was in order and could run itself easily for the next three months, Walter replied, "Hell, Clarence, our boys moved in yesterday".

1935 saw another complete re-style for the division. Dodge fared better than most of the corporation through the 'Airflow' debacle of the early part of the 1930s, mainly because the planned introduction of the futuristically-styled cars was quickly abandoned for Dodge (and Plymouth) when early sales figures of Airflow DeSotos and Chryslers showed that the buying public had rejected the new style wholeheartedly. However, a Dodge Airflow truck was introduced in 1934 and the watered-down Airstream styling came to all corporation cars eventually. As can be seen on this 1937 Series D5 four-door touring sedan, every panel had been smoothed out for a very curvaceous look – not an Airflow, but not a million miles away from it either.

Indeed they had. Chrysler's production expert K T Keller, along with a team of executives, had already moved in and informed E J Wilmer that he and his team were no longer required. Previously prepared signs reading 'Chrysler Corporation – Dodge Division' started to appear almost immediately, and when the plant opened for business the next morning Dodge was under complete Chrysler control, with K T Keller becoming the first Dodge Division President. The latest Chrysler Division, now without the 'Brothers' suffix in its title, grew rapidly and rose from 13th in the US motor industry to 7th in just one year. By 1933, it had risen to 4th, just behind Chrysler's Plymouth brand.

So were set the foundations for Chrysler's Dodge Division, and we now know where Dodge came from and how, with its supreme craftsmanship and attention to detail, Dodge acquired its name for ruggedness and dependability. But I think that it is time that we talked about its performance cars, and to do this we have to move quickly on to post-World War II.

Lee Petty, 1954. Petty began a family business that continues to this day. Starting with Plymouth, he campaigned little cars until Dodge brought out its Hemi engine. Petty then swapped right away. In 1953 he took his V8-powered Dodge to its first win at the first race of that season. This was Dodge Division's first ever Grand National stock car victory.

Dodge had been building on its reputation for reliability throughout the Depression, and, along with other car manufacturers, gave stalwart service during the war years of the forties. It was Dodge that built the Wright cyclone engines for B-29 heavy bombers, including the Enola Gay aircraft that dropped the first A-bomb on Japan in 1945. Dodge factories also built over half a million military trucks and numerous other pieces of hardware for the war effort. But now, lots of Americans were coming home from service in the forces, looking to build on what they had fought for. The great 'American Dream' was to prosper, have a job, own a home and drive your own car, and this they did, in great numbers.

When the US Government authorised conversion of factories from military back to civilian production in July of 1945, a race was on to build as many cars as possible. Within weeks, Ford had new cars back in its dealerships, but Dodge, along with the rest of the Chrysler Corporation, got off to a very slow start. Due to labour problems, material shortages, unfinished war contracts and converting factories back to civilian production, Dodge made fewer than 500 cars by the end of that year, and it wasn't until later in 1946 that full production returned.

The cars produced between 1946 and 1949 were almost identical to the pre-war models. The public's voracious appetite for new cars meant that no manufacturer in the US could make them fast enough. As the decade drew to a close and life started to settle down somewhat, the buying public became more choosy, turning away from cars that only offered mechanical reliability towards those that offered reliability, modern styling and performance. No Chrysler

1942 Dodge DeLuxe. This was the last of the pre-war models; Dodge introduced the Deluxe and Custom with another facelift of the 1940 bodies. This consisted mainly of an elaborate but bigger grille and front wing, molded running board and an abundance of chrome trim. A larger 230.2in³ 6-cylinder engine boosted horsepower to 105 from the previous year's 91bhp. All '42s rode on a 119½ inch wheelbase. The beautifully proportioned 2-door (long-deck) business coupé shown here was the cheapest car from Dodge that year, but still only attracted 5237 buyers and sold for $895. When the war was over and Dodge returned to civilian production with its 1946 models, very little changed. All Chrysler vehicles went without any major updates until 1949.

Corporation cars offered this. Buyers turned away in their thousands and headed for the new stylish Ford and General Motors cars. The man largely held responsible for this policy was K T Keller, Dodge's first divisional President in 1928, and by then President of the Chrysler Corporation. The utilitarian 3-box styling that had been promoted by Keller since before the war, now seemed incredibly dated. Famed for quotes such as "I want a car I can wear my hat in", and "people want reliability not style", illustrated his anachronistic vision. But Keller can also take much of the credit for saving Chrysler too, because he did one very important thing: he hired a stylist named Virgil Exner, and that one action was about to turn the American automotive world on its head.

CHRYSLER FINDS STYLE

Virgil Exner had been working at the now famed Raymond Loewy design studios since the late 1930s, after a brief stint at GM. Virgil's talents soon became obvious and he was put in charge of the recently acquired Studebaker account. Exner was just in time to put the finishing touches to the '39 Champion and develop the 1941 series. Throughout the war, Exner designed many vehicles including amphibious Weasels, DUKWs, and other military trucks. But Virgil wasn't happy at Loewy's Studio. He disagreed with Loewy's habit of taking the credit for his younger designers' efforts. Work had begun on the first new post-war Studebaker as early as 1944. Loewy's team had a design but Virgil, in his spare time, came up with an alternative. Studebaker management preferred Virgil's to Loewy's. This would become the famous 1947 model, with its amazing rear three piece wrap-around windshield that gave the impression of a car with two front ends.

Loewy saw this as a betrayal and fired Exner. But within 24 hours, Exner had been set up with his own design group, working on a separate Studebaker account. At this time he styled the 1950 line, but Loewy still had a lot of influence at Studebaker and the aeroplane front end of Loewy's won through. So the '50 became a mix between the two styling groups. This would be the last Stude project for Exner.

In 1949 K T Keller hired Exner to head the new Advanced Styling Studio at Chrysler. This department had nothing to do with Chrysler's production cars at all, which were still being taken care of by corporate design-chief Henry King, Virgil's boss. Exner was assigned the task of designing a new parade phaeton, along with a series of 'concept' or 'idea cars'.

These cars, designed by Exner and built by Ghia in Turin, Italy, are now legendary, with the K310 perhaps the most famous. Exner's love of Italian styling was well known, so the partnership worked well.

Virgil M Exner was the stylist that stopped the downward slide in sales for the Chrysler Corporation. His elegant idea cars from the early 1950s led to his involvement with the production cars. His '100 Million Dollar Look' of 1955 and the second generation 'Forward Look' from 1957 stole the styling lead from General Motors for many years. However, Exner said that his greatest achievement from that period was not the cars that he designed, but rather the creation of the styling organization at Chrysler.

Even the conservative K T Keller was impressed. So much so, that Exner was finally let loose on the production car design. Exner, now Director of Styling, along with his small team of Maury Baldwin, Cliff Voss and Ted Pietsch were in time to make small changes to the 1954 models. But sales were slipping dramatically. In a major shake up, K T Keller was 'promoted' to Chairman of the Board and was replaced as President by forward thinking Lester Lum 'Tex' Colbert.

'Tex' Colbert realized the importance of styling and immediately took steps to be rid of Keller's stodgy 3-box design. With a production led-time of just two years, Exner was given the huge task of completely re-styling the 1955 models, and as we will see, this he did to great effect. But we mustn't get ahead of ourselves here. Something else happened at Chrysler in the early fifties that would help shape Dodge into what it is today. It was the introduction of arguably the most famous engine in the world. The legendary Hemi V8.

1951 Chrysler NewYorker. Now things really started to heat up in the power war. Chrysler introduced its new hemispherical ('Hemi') head Firepower V8 engine. Other makers were introducing V8s but none could touch the Hemi. Racers and auto manufacturers all took note. Chrysler had been working on an engine design that would run on cheaper fuels but with no loss in power. It achieved this and quite a bit more. The basic configuration allowed for major upgrading and extra power was the result. This 1951 Chrysler NewYorker convertible helped herald the arrival of the new Firepower V8, when Chrysler was awarded the honor of pacing the Indy 500 race in May of that year.

THE EARLY HEMI 1951

In 1945 James C Zeder, along with a small engineering research team, started trying to produce an automobile engine with a hemispherical-shaped combustion chamber. This was not a new invention, and had been tried in Europe and America with some success for many years. The team had already designed a V16 Hemi engine for use in fighter aircraft. But Zeder wanted to take the Hemi a huge step further. To design an engine that would yield maximum power with minimum effort, and be reliable enough to go into a regular production car. It had to be good enough to replace Chrysler's almost indestructible side-valve L-head 8 and 6-cylinder engines. After six years of research, what they came up with was nothing short of an engineering masterpiece: the Firepower V8.

The 331in³ Firepower Hemi V8 debuted to much acclaim in the 1951 Chrysler line. A modified version also appeared in Virgil Exner's 1951 K310 show car. The engine came standard on all but the base Windsor models, which still came with the 116hp L-head 6. No other corporate marques received the new V8. It had taken time but Zeder's team now had a proven power plant that would achieve exceptional volumetric efficiency matched with totally outstanding performance, while relying on a lower compression ratio. All this using a lower octane fuel than the competitors 'non-Hemied' engines. The Hemi got its name from 'hemispherical', but the combustion chambers are technically called spherical segment or lenticular-shaped. Nevertheless, the slang name stuck.

But what made the Hemi so good? Its design incorporated several revolutionary features. The then unique combination of the wedge shape combustion chamber and overhead valve arrangement made the engine very compact, but also led to other advantages – mainly that the sparkplugs could be positioned in the center of the chambers, offering better combustion of the gases and higher thermal efficiency. This allowed more room for larger valves spaced further apart, which in turn supplied faster and better refilling of the combustion chambers with the fuel and air mixture. The design also allowed smoother porting and manifolding, larger coolant passages and low heat rejection through the coolant. This enabled Chrysler to utilize a smaller, lighter radiator. The downside to all of this was that the motor was very expensive to produce.

Racers and hot rodders were very quick to see the potential of the new engine. Chrysler itself backed cars in 1952 when Hemi-powered Saratoga's were entered in the NASCAR stock-car racing series. American millionaire Briggs Cunningham also used the new Chrysler V8 to power his C2-Rs for the 1951 Le Mans endurance race, and went on to have modest success in later years with his Hemi powered C-4R and C-5R cars. In 1952 a special version was tested in a Kurtis-Kraft Indy roadster, but incredibly was banned by racing officials as too fast. Although very expensive to build, the huge initial success of the Hemi spurred Chrysler on to think about introducing the engine to other corporate marques. In 1952, DeSoto brought out the new Firedome series, powered of course by a Firedome Hemi V8. And in 1953, Dodge received its own: the Red Ram V8.

This 1951 picture shows the diversity of vehicles that Dodge was up against. Al Teague in his number 6 Hudson Hornet is at the top, in the middle is a streamline Nash, and at the bottom is Indy driver Johnny Mantz in his number 98 1950 Plymouth fastback, two-door sedan. Mantz won the first ever 500 mile stock car race, the Southern 500, using this little sedan.

1953 Diplomat, the first performance car from Dodge. It is rather tame-looking, perhaps, but looks can be deceptive. The Jet-Flow air scoop sitting under the Ram mascot gives away the secret that this car was fitted with Dodge's all-new Red Ram Hemi V8 engine. The 241.3in³ motor gave an advertised (but almost definitely understated) 140bhp at 4400rpm. This engine – matched with the lightweight body of the Diplomat coupé – was a powerful combination. Racing driver Danny Eames took one of these cars to a new record of 102.6mph at El Mirage in California in '53 but, just as impressive, Dodge won its class in the 1953 running of the Mobilgas Economy Run using a four-door Coronet fitted with the Red Ram V8.

RED RAM 1953

On 30 May 1950, the green flag fell on the first NASCAR race that included a Dodge in the field. The place was Canfield Motor Speedway, Canfield, Ohio, and the driver was Carl Wilkerson, who finished 25th that day out of 29 starters. Momentous but not successful, and in Dodge dealerships, sales were in a serious downward dive. Forward-thinking 'Tex' Colbert gave the go ahead for Exner to do what he could to enhance the styling of the 1953 and 1954 models, which had already been designed. What came about was not breath-taking, and compared to the competition at the time, still tall and dated, but even so, the 1953 Dodges were not bad looking cars. In fact, to be fair, some of the '53 models were very attractive. Curved one-piece windshield, a lower hood and more integral rear fenders all helped to give these cars a smoother more modern appearance. But it was the mechanical side of Dodge that shone through again, and this time turned the motoring world on its

head. A new double channel 'Road-Action' chassis was introduced, along with a refined suspension set-up. Also new was the 'Gyro-Torque Drive' automatic transmission, operated by lifting the foot off the accelerator instead of depressing the clutch. However, the big news was what the transmission was bolted to. In 1953

Dodge received its own version of the already famous Hemi V8 and Dodge's name for dependability was just about to be overshadowed by a new name for PERFORMANCE!

Dubbed the Red Ram, the Dodge Hemi was actually smaller than either the Chrysler or DeSoto Firedome version – but Dodge would make the most of this powerful new weapon. Almost at once Dodge had become a major contender in the new power battle that had started to gain momentum since the end of the war. It is important to note that Dodge got its V8 a good two years ahead of Plymouth, indicative of the

1953 Red Ram V8. Used extensively in advertising at the time, the Red Ram V8 engine was in fact a scaled-down version of Chrysler's 331in³ Hemi-head V8. Only available in the Coronet Series, this engine gained an enviable reputation for durability and performance. Like its big 331in³ brother, the Red Ram took advantage of its unique combination of wedge-shaped combustion chambers and overhead valve arrangement to allow for optimum usage of the motor. Dodge press releases at the time claimed the Red Ram to be "the most efficient engine design in any American car!" They pretty much had it right.

All new '53 Dodge. Almost all Dodge advertising was aimed at the performance-minded professional. It was deemed socially unacceptable to have a weak car and almost all the emphasis was on jet-flow, pilot view, high-flying gadgetry and gimmicks as the world entered the jet-age.

performance emphasis that was now being placed on Dodge, and which still holds true today. The Red Ram engine, with its 241.3in³ displacement, gave 140bhp. Small indeed, compared to Chrysler's 180bhp 331.1 Hemi and DeSoto's 160 horsepower 276.1in³ V8, but still, placed in the new lightweight Dodge, it flew. It was lighter and smaller than Chrysler and DeSoto, but more importantly, lighter, quicker and cheaper than its three main rivals: the Oldsmobile 88, the '53 Mercury and the Hudson Hornet.

There were three series in this year from Dodge – the Meadowbrook Special, the Meadowbrook, and the Coronet. The new V8 engine was

1953 Dodge. The style of the '53 was not very impressive and it was almost bland compared to its rivals, but just two years down the line Dodge would become a style leader. This four-door Coronet sedan is typical of the kind of car that all Chrysler divisions were making. New for Dodge were integrated front and rear fenders, a curved one-piece front windshield and a hidden centerpost on four-door models, all of which helped to make the cars more modern-looking than the previous year's offerings. Dodge had started hunting for a share in a new market – the 'young buyer'.

only made available to the top range Coronets. Aimed mainly at the travelling salesman market, Meadowbrook Specials were for all intents and purposes very basic Coronets, coming with few standard features, a lack of exterior side trim and sparse interiors. The Specials would be discontinued later that year and replaced by the Meadowbrook series, allowing room for a new top of the range model to be introduced mid-1954 season, the Royal. Identification was very simple between the models. All cars fitted with a V8 had a 'Jet-Flow' air scoop fitted to the front of the hood, on which sat a large chrome 'V' with the words DODGE and EIGHT on either side. The Coronet name also appeared in chrome script on the sides of the front fenders. The Meadowbrook Specials and Meadowbrook series had much simpler hoods that carried the Dodge crest as a centerpiece. All 1953 cars had a larger chrome 'Ram' ornament on top of the hood.

Cross-section of the 1953 V8. This picture of the 241.3in^3 Hemi shows clearly (on the left bank) how the sparkplug sits in a more central location in the dome-shaped chamber. The right bank shows the overhead valves. This layout left the engine better prepared for modifications.

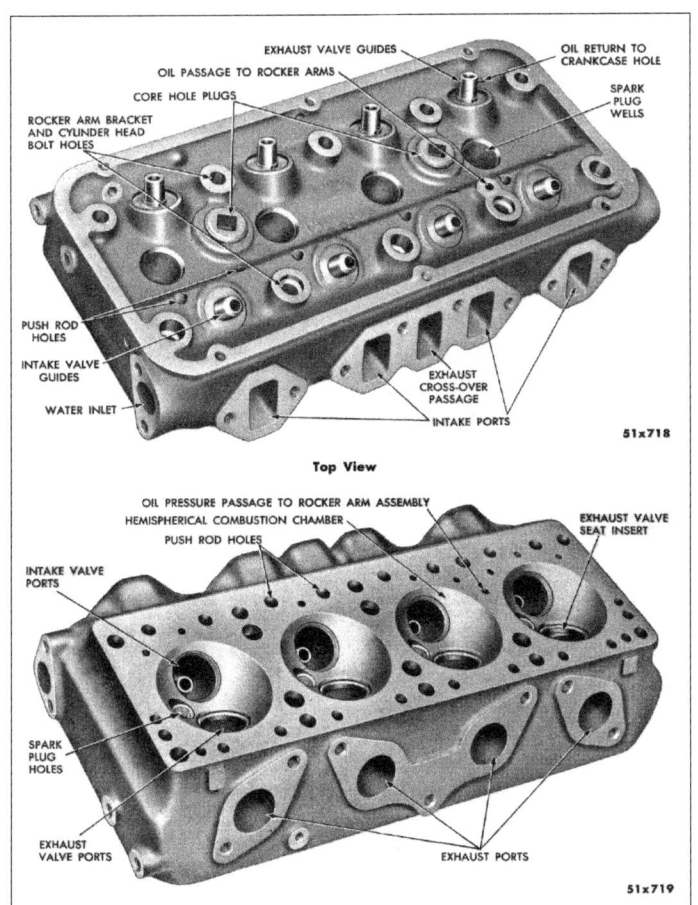

This cutaway is of the Dodge Hemi cylinder head, taken from the '53 workshop manual. It clearly shows the unusually shaped lenticular or hemispherical (Hemi) combustion chambers that allowed for overhead valves and larger water jacket. This was an expensive engine to build which was replaced by a 'Polyspherical' head a few years later.

1953 Diplomat. Aside from the Coronet convertible, this two-door Coronet Diplomat coupé was as stylish as you could get from Dodge in 1953. This photograph, taken in a dealer's showroom, demonstrates how optional extras were used to sell the cars to the young and young-at-heart. Kelsey Hayes wire wheels, white-wall tires, dual exhausts and factory continental spare wheel were just some of the options available. And, of course, there was that all-important Hemi V8.

The performance versions of the 1953 Dodge were definitely the Coronet Diplomat, which was a 2-door six passenger hardtop coupé, and the Coronet convertible, the main reasoning for this being the shorter 114in wheelbase used on these two models (along with the Suburban station wagon) compared to 119in for the remaining models, giving a major weight saving. It didn't take long for professional racers to pick up on this. The Coronets went head to head with Ford and GM cars across the United States with great success. In California, Dodge Chief Test Driver Danny Eames took a '53 to a new record of 102.6mph at El Mirage dry lake. Incredibly though, the Dodge V8s also won their class in the Mobilgas Economy Runs for 1953, averaging 23.4mpg. In stock car racing, Lee Petty proved just how good the Dodge combination was in

the very first race of the 1953 season, held at the Palm Beach Speedway in Palm Beach, Florida. On lap 49 of the 200-lap race, Petty found himself leading the pack, and that is where he remained until the checkered flag. Lee Petty had won Dodge's first ever Grand National stock car victory.

Along with four other wins and 25 top five finishes in the 1953 season, this was enough to give him second place in the points chase, just behind Herb Thomas, who won the championship in a Hudson.

The following year saw a handsome but mild facelift, which relied mainly on a heavier grill and side trim and very small but significant chrome fins. The first to be seen on a Dodge, but boy would they grow! Horsepower also grew, to 150bhp from the same 241in^3. Dodge celebrated its 40th birthday in this year and to help celebrate

this, along with its new found name for performance, a 1954 Dodge was selected to pace the prestigious Indianapolis 500 mile motor race.

The Indy 500 Pace Cars were convertibles from the new top of the range Royal series, which had been introduced in October of '54. Only two real Pace Cars were made. These both had every electrical connection soldered to minimise the risk of an embarrassing breakdown half way around the famous Brickyard track, along with blue printed engines. Only available with the new V8 engine, 701 Pace Car replicas were made. They all matched the real Pace Car with pale yellow bodywork and a host of standard equipment taken from the 1954 options list – Continental kit, dual exhausts and Kelsey Hayes wire wheels all went on these 'specials'. Some were even fitted with an Offenhauser manifold setup for extra performance.

1954 Pace Car. Dodge changed very little for 1954; the biggest news was the introduction of a new series, the Royal. This took over from the Coronet as top of the range. The same 241in³ Hemi V8 was made available in all Dodges, and the engine capacity had grown to 150bhp. For the first time in its forty-year history it was selected to pace the Indy 500 race. A fully loaded Royal convertible was used, complete with continental kit and wire wheels. A limited edition run of replica Pace Cars was built. All were convertibles, and all were painted in the same yellow with Pace Car markings. These were called Royal 500s. These 701 replicas were fitted with 'Pace Car Engines' (V8s with four-barrel Carter carbs instead of the standard Stromberg two-barrel), and twin exhausts with special fanned tips. Here you see actors Jerry Lewis and Dean Martin helping to celebrate the Indy 500.

This 1953 advertisement played down performance, and used the thrifty economy and safety aspects of the car to appeal to the more conservative buyer.

1955 Custom Royal. All change for 1955 with the introduction of Virgil Exner's 'Forward Look'. These cars, along with Plymouth, DeSoto, Imperial and Chrysler, took the public by storm and Chrysler's rivals by surprise. The '55s were longer, lower, wider and sportier than any mass-produced car yet built in America. Full wrap-around windshields, subtle use of chrome trim, triple-tone paint schemes, and more powerful V8 engines were all part of the recipe that helped make 1955 a great year for Dodge.

THE 100 MILLION DOLLAR LOOK

The effect that unveiling the 1955 Chrysler Corporation cars had on the automotive world, and the general public, should not be underestimated. Remember this was in the 'good old days', when an unveiling meant just that. New cars were kept under wraps in dealerships after being delivered. Some deliveries were even made in the dead of night to keep everybody guessing until the very last minute. The excitement for locals, adults and children alike, was always high as this used to be a major event in towns the length and breadth of America.

On November 17 1954, the covers were lifted on a series of cars that turned people's attitudes towards Chrysler around completely. Gone were the tall, stodgy, drab cars of pre-war America. In their place stood low, wide, colorful powerhouse cars that brought dealer showrooms to life. Virgil Exner's designs had stolen the styling leadership away from GM in one fell swoop, and caused a sensation.

Almost every manufacturer had a boom year in 1955, but the Chrysler Corporation's was exceptional. Virgil Exner's 'Forward Look' was introduced as 'The 100 Million Dollar Look', as an indication of the reputed cost of retooling for these new cars. The new Dodge, with its 'Flair-Fashion' styling, was arguably the best-looking Dodge yet. The public agreed and production soared from the 1954 total of 154,648 to 276,936 units in '55. It was over 6.5in longer than the previous year's offerings – wider and lower, but still recognizably Dodge.

The designs were actually penned by Maury Baldwin, one of Exner's design team, along the same lines as Virgil's Chrysler, Imperial and DeSoto (Baldwin also designed the Plymouth). A reworking of the '54 grill ran up to a lower hood and the browed headlights. Gone was the Ram hood ornament, making way for a more stylized, lower chrome centerpiece that spread out across the front of the hood and worked its way back to the door pillars. From here, it followed the side of the body,

dipping down on some models just after the front doors to form a 'V', before ending at the rear light bezels. This lent itself very well to the bright new tri-tone and two-tone paint schemes that were coming out. From the thirteen basic colors available, any combination could be had. A fuller wraparound 'new horizon' front windshield gave a more panoramic view of the road, and the Powerflite automatic transmission control lever had moved from the steering column to the dash. All '55s fitted with a V8 had a large chrome 'V' on the front of the hood, under the Dodge coat of arms.

Three engines were available in 1955. Still going strong was the in-line 'Getaway Six' as a base engine, the Red Ram V8 and the new Super Red Ram. The Red Ram and Super Red Ram shared the same cast iron block and had the same 270in³ displacement, but the Red Ram used a new 'Polyspherical' head with a single rocker shaft. Cheaper to build than the Hemi, with a compression ratio of 7.6:1, it gave 175bhp at 4400rpm. This was the standard engine on all Royals and optional on Coronets.

The Super Red Ram still made use of the Hemi-head with its double rocker shafts. With the same 2-barrel Stromberg carb that the Poly-head engine used, the Super Red Ram gave 183bhp at 4400rpm. With the optional Carter 4 barrel and twin exhaust setup, horsepower increased to a formidable 193. It was a winning package with the public, but the winning didn't stop at the dealership doors.

MOTORSPORT 1953-1959

From the outset, Dodge started to chalk up successes, but it wasn't having it all its own way. There was competition and lots of it. But what was the competition, and how did Dodge get involved with organized motorsport?

Official stock car motor racing developed from the bootleggers who used to run moonshine whiskey in the depression. These bootleggers needed fast cars and quick wits to out-pace the police, and they also raced each other. What they generally used were Fords, heavily modified but still recognizable as Fords. As motor racing became more popular and more legitimate, several organizations thought to set down ground rules. The AAA (American Automobile Association) and ACA (Automobile Club of America) were just two of many local and national bodies that had their own differing rules. Almost all of these were first and foremost motoring organizations, with nothing specifically to do with racing. But in 1947 a man named Bill (William) France, part time racer, mechanic and promoter, went about setting up something that would become quite unique. A sanctioning body that would exist purely for racing. It was named the National Association for Stock Car Auto Racing (NASCAR).

The first strictly stock car race run under the new NASCAR guidelines was in June 1949. The term 'stock car' was very loose, by the way. Those same Ford coupes from the late 30s ran with full fenders and a windshield, a production gas tank and standard ignition, but that was about it. Any engine could be used with any modifications the engine could handle, including any heads and carbs that would work. These first cars were classed as 'Modifieds', and had just the barest resemblance to stock production cars. But it didn't take long for auto manufacturers to realize that their cars winning races helped to sell production cars. Manufacturers made it increasingly easy for racers and promoters to get their hands on newer production cars. The early Fords were undeniably fast, but advances in fuel and engine design throughout the war meant that the fresher, more efficient, but mainly more powerful engines were being debuted. GM's five divisions all went at this separately, Chrysler was also developing a V8, and the independent makers were in there too. By 1950-51, Ford was left flagging in the horsepower race. First out of the box was GM's Oldsmobile in 1949, with its Rocket 88. This V8 gave 136bhp from its 303in³ displacement, and it really was a rocket! Next was Cadillac's new V8, but the car was too expensive for stock car racing. Chrysler joined the party in 1951 with the new Firepower engine, as did Hudson, with its Hornet. Although still using only a side-valve 6 engine, the Hudson motor had a massive 308in³ that offered huge amounts of torque. The Hornet was much lower and more streamlined than the other cars. Along with the lightweight little Plymouths with their straight 6s, these were the main contenders.

On the track at least, it was Hudson that ruled the roost in the early 50s, winning the NASCAR manufacturers title in 1951, 1952 and 1953. With its 'export' (read racing) options that satisfied NASCAR regulations, it was the first (but not the only) major backer of professional stock car racing, producing optional performance parts which were listed in its catalogues as standard export or heavy-duty equipment. Unfortunately, when Hudson merged with Nash in 1954, this ended Hudson's racing interests almost completely.

So this was the competition that Dodge was up against in 1953. Professional stock car racing was young and exciting and as it spread from its southern roots, across America, it picked up momentum and found racers, promoters, fans and manufacturers all wanting to jump on the bandwagon. When Dodge introduced the Hemi into its lightweight cars, there was almost a mass exodus of drivers from Plymouth to Dodge, one of whom was Lee Petty. Petty, racing under the #42, had already captured Plymouth's first Grand National win and now did the same for Dodge when he won the first race of the season at Palm Beach, Florida. Petty took another four wins that season, along with a win for Dodge driver Dick Meyer and numerous top ten finishes.

Everyone at Dodge knew that the 1953 models were quick, but what to do about it? Sales Manager Bert Carter hired experienced racing driver Danny Eames as Chief Test Driver for Dodge, and because of the car's initial success, a performance program was put in place that gave Eames 'an open ticket' from William Newberg, Dodge Division President, to take on whatever trials he saw fit that would enhance Dodge's performance image. Newberg already saw Dodge as the performance division of Chrysler.

This adventurous program which included the Daytona Speedweek, Endurance Trials, California's tough

Highway Patrol Acceptance Test and even the Pikes Peak Hill Climb were all undertaken successfully, mainly because of the enthusiasm of three men: William C Newberg, R D (Dean) Engle, Chief Engineer and Danny Eames.

A factory-backed team used a 1954 Dodge to set no less than 196 AAA stock car speed records at Bonneville Salt Flats in Utah, in September of 1953. And although the big Lincolns are famous for ruling it, Dodge cars swept the board in the treacherous Carrera PanAmerica (Mexican Road Race) coming in 1-2-3-4-6-9 in the Medium Stock Class – a level of success that even Lincoln couldn't match. Even Dodge's Firearrow convertible show car proved its worth, when it set a new woman's world speed record of 143.44mph on the 4.7 mile oval test track at Chryslers new Chelsea Proving Ground. In addition, across America, the Dodges were taking the checkered flags with owner/driver teams.

But the most high profile racer of this period must be Carl Kiekhaefer. Kiekhaefer was an industrialist who liked to win. Best known for running Chrysler 300s, Kiekhaefer also used Dodge, and his was perhaps the first factory-backed race team as we think of it today. He owned Mercury Outboard Motors and to advertise his products, Mercury Outboard was painted on the side of all his race cars in big red letters. Confusing for some when they first saw an all white Dodge or Chrysler tear past with Mercury written all over it!

Kiekhaefer had no loyalty to any automaker. He used whatever was fastest at the time and best suited to the race, along with some of the best racers around – drivers like Tim and Fonty Flock, Buck Baker and Frank Mundy. His Ford and Lincoln cars soon fell by the wayside when Chrysler released the Hemi in 1951. Working closely with Chrysler engineers, Carl helped a great deal to develop the engine for racing. It was in fact the Kiekhaefer factory that

later supplied Dodge with prototype intakes for the 56 D-500-1, and Dean Engle states that it was also Carl who suggested the dual quad intake and carb setup that found its way to the race version.

His theory on how to win was basically flooding the track with fast cars. If one of them didn't win, another of his team probably would. And whereas most racers drove their cars to the track, Carl had trailers, spare wheels/tires and a large pit team. By 1955, Kiekhaefer was fielding a mix of 300Bs and Dodge 2-door sedans. This factory-backed big money strategy worked. In the 1955 NASCAR season there were 45 Grand National races and Chrysler cars took 27 of them. Kiekhaefer's Tim Flock took 18 of them by himself A record that stands unbeaten today! This strategy worked so well that it prompted Ford and Chevrolet to all-out war for the next season. This really was the start of the muscle car power war.

Danny Eames, one of the most important people behind Dodge's success in the early 1950s. Danny was the Chief Test Driver at Dodge and was, of course, an experienced racing driver. Between 1953 and 1956 he was given carte blanche to decide which competitions Dodge cars should enter in order to promote the company's new performance image. Daytona Speedweeks, Bonneville endurance trials, Pikes Peak hill climbs, and even the California Highway Patrol acceptance tests were just some of the events completed with great success by Danny. He is pictured here (left) with Dodge racing driver Marvin Panch after another success in the 1954 Dodge.

Styling for '56. Building on the success of the styling used on 1955 cars, the '56 facelifts were well done. A slightly more intricate grille at the front led around to a side trim that dipped sharply at the rear of the car. This helped accentuate the tri-tone and two-tone paint schemes. But it was the fins that really made an impression – not just a chrome afterthought, these aircraft-like tails started just over halfway down the body and gradually rose to a chrome-tipped peak. Set within the fins were 'twin-jet taillights' and with optional dual jet-like exhaust tips. The whole package told the buyer that this was a car that would really fly down the freeway!

DODGE D-500

"It's a real bomb!", claimed Dodge advertising about the new D-500. And that pretty much covered it. This was, by design, the first true Dodge performance car. Based on the facelift of the '55 models, this was, in terms of looks at least, nothing more than a normal production car. But under the hood ... that was something else. Sitting on a special double-channelled, heavy-duty box section chassis that used Chrysler New Yorker parts, was the biggest power plant ever seen thus far in a Dodge production model – a redesigned 315in^3 Hemi V8 which gave out a whopping 260 horsepower. To stop this machine, 12in drum brakes taken from the senior Chrysler models were utilized, along with other heavy-duty suspension parts from Imperials.

These cars had phenomenal success on the track and the strip, but nowadays are a forgotten breed – but why? When the 1956 cars were debuted, each Chrysler Division had its own 'sports car'. Plymouth had

'It's a real bomb!' – the 1956 D-500. Dodge's forgotten muscle car is usually described as being just a performance option which is a great misconception. As with DeSoto's Adventurer, Plymouth's Fury and Chrysler's 300 series, the Dodge D-500 was without doubt a series in its own right. Misinformation through the years, along with misleading or inaccurate publicity at the time, didn't help the D-500 with its 'identity crisis'. It was launched on 22 December 1955 and took its name from the Indy 500 race, the next step from the Royal 500 Pace Car of 1954. On 12 January 1956, Dodge announced the D-500-1 racing version. An optional performance package was later introduced using standard Dodge equipment but with the D-500 engine. These were known as D-500 Specials. The Specials were available across the Dodge range from 9 March 1956, and it was this more than anything else that robbed the true D-500s of their proper place in motoring history.

1956 D-500. The 1953 Dodge Diplomat and '54 Pace Car were performance models more by luck than judgment on Dodge's part, but the 1956 D-500 was a pure factory hot-rod, Dodge's first thoroughbred muscle car. From inception to design and final production, this car was built to race. Sitting on a 120in heavy-duty chassis, these cars had larger exhausts, larger 12in drum brakes, heavy-duty suspension and the vital Hemi V8 mill. They were only available as Coronet two-door sedans, Custom Royal two-door coupes or Custom Royal convertibles, and the only outward distinguishing feature (other than lower suspension) was the D-500 checkered flag badge on the front of the hood, which can be seen on this Custom Royal Lancer.

Super Red Ram engine. Released in late 1955 for the 1956 models, the already powerful Red Ram mill had been tweaked from 193bhp with its 270.1in³ up to 218bhp from an enlarged 315in³ mill. This engine, now called the Super Red Ram, was fitted as standard equipment on all Royal and Custom Royal models. D-500 buyers got a whooping 230bhp (from a single 4-barrel carb) or 260bhp (with dual 4-barrel carbs) from the same 315in³ engine.

the Fury, DeSoto had the Adventurer, and of course Chrysler had its 300B. All came with distinctive trim and exclusive paint-schemes. Dodge did the same thing and released the D-500. What differed though was the styling of the cars and the way they were advertised. The D-500 was limited in its availability, with just the Coronet 2-door hardtop, Custom Royal 2-door coupé or Custom Royal convertible being used, but only had a 'suggested' paint scheme of Oriental Coral and Sapphire White (customers could order any color from the Dodge paint range at extra cost). The only outward signs that the cars were different from other 'bread and butter' models was the lower rear end due to the heavy-duty suspension, and the small D-500 checkered flag badge on the front of the hood. It also didn't help the D-500s identity crisis when shortly after its release, Dodge – wanting to cash in on extra sales – announced a D-500 power option available on all models. This watered down power-pack used standard Dodge mechanics. Even more confusing was a D-500 Special, which was any Dodge, but fitted with a D-500 engine. All of this helped people believe that the initial D-500 was just an option package and not a series in its own right, as it most surely was. Articles in magazines like *Hot Rod* (May 1956) gave inaccurate information, while poorly worded advertising from Dodge only helped to bury the model. But the people who built the car should know, right? Bert Carter, Sales Manager said in a letter of December 1955, "You will note the units are priced as D-500 models – complete and not as a package of extra equipment". Also, Dodge President William C Newberg, Chief Test Driver Danny Eames, and Dean Engle, Chief Engineer, have all stated that the D-500 "was without a doubt a model and not an option package". You can't get much better than that.

Of all the stock car racing outfits from the 1950s, Carl Kiekhaefer's Mercury Outboard Team must surely be the most famous. Kiekhaefer was an industrialist who owned Mercury Outboards but he also liked to race, and for him winning was everything. Kiekhaefer had no loyalty to any auto manufacturer but always ran the fastest cars available. To this end, when Chrysler released the Hemi engine he dropped his favored Lincolns for the new cars. These are two of the team's cars – a Chrysler 300B waiting next to a Dodge D-500-1 ready for the off.

Still in the thick of it, this is Kiekhaefer's D-500-1 (no 502) keeping with the pack in the 1956 race season but led by a '56 Ford and '56 Chevy.

Special mention must be made here of the D-500-1. The racers of the day like Kiekhaefer, Lee Petty and Danny Eames were all requesting more power for their race cars. The D-500-1 was a factory built extra-heavy-duty vehicle, 'for racing only'. Available only as a Coronet 2-door sedan or convertible with manual transmission, these cars eventually came equipped with extra H-D chassis and suspension, reworked wheelarches to allow for the special 8.5in wide rims, a blue-printed engine with a hot cam and a special dual quad carb and aluminum intake setup. In its initial form the D-500-1 was good for 276bhp. Although no exact figures exist, it is understood that no more than 100 D-500-1 (for racing only) cars were built, along with one prototype D-500-2 which was built at Highland Park for Carl Kiekhaefer, and used a 354in³ Chrysler 300B engine.

1956 D-500 convertible. Although renowned for not being the easiest man to get on with and a hard disciplinarian, Carl Kiekhaefer looked after his drivers and paid them well. Some of NASCAR's most famous drivers raced for Carl at some point, among them Buck Baker, Charles Scott, Speedy Thompson and Tim and Fonty Flock. This is Frank Mundy, winner of the 1955 Daytona Beach race (in a Chrysler 300), next to his team Dodge convertible. Kiekhaefer usually fielded two-door sedans but when a class for convertibles appeared he went for that, too.

Another D-500 convertible, this time raced by Marvin Panch. No roll bars are fitted; a simple vinyl jacket covers the cabin to help with airflow. The badges and lights were simply taped over and a wire mesh was placed over the front bumper and grille to deflect gravel from hitting the bumpers or radiator.

The racers most favored by William Newberg had these cars given to them. Lee Petty and Carl Kiekhaefer were just two of the recipients. Almost anything they wanted, they got, but it isn't widely known that this arrangement didn't last, and may in some way have helped Kiekhaefer make his decision to retire at the end of the '56 season.

When Byron J Nichols, Vice President at Dodge, was given the job of handling the Kiekhaefer program for 1957, he promptly organized a meeting with Carl and some other necessary staff. After discussing at length Kiekhaefer's requirements for cars, equipment and transportation, Mr Nichols asked Kiekhaefer how he would like to pay for his order. "PAY?! I don't pay for anything!" came the angry response. This is when it came out that Kiekhaefer had been givien carte blanche while dealing with William Newberg. Nichols excused himself from the meeting for a quick discussion with Newberg. Newberg told Nichols that yes, this had been the case but that he (Nichols) was now in charge and should make the decision as to whether Dodge should continue to carry Carl's efforts. Returning to the meeting Carl's last words before leaving were: "When

you're ready to deliver the equipment, let me know." Nichols replied with: "When you decide how to pay for it let me know." So ended the Kiekhaefer/ Dodge relationship, but Kiekhaefer's team did go on and win the national title for '56.

The D-500s and D-500-1s took a whole host of wins and set records in all fields of motorsport. As early as September 1955 Danny Eames,

This D-500-1 is rumored to be the last surviving example of the model. Only 100 were ever made, and because of the harsh life that they led, most were destroyed. This car was specially ordered by a racing driver but was never raced, hence its fantastic condition today.

D-500 badge. The crossed checkered flag badge found on the hood and trunk is the only outward sign that this is not your everyday Dodge production model.

Daytona Speedweek. If proof were needed of the Dodge D-500's performance, then NASCAR's Speedweek at Daytona Beach provided it. Dodge Chief Test Driver Danny Eames took a D-500 to a new acceleration record with a flying mile of 81.786mph, beating all the other US production cars from all classes. Dodge also came in third (Dean Martin in a '56 D-500) and fourth places (Howard Palmer in a '55 Dodge). Eames also set a new mark for the two-way flying mile when he achieved an average for the two runs of 130.577mph. Daytona's hard-packed sand was almost perfect for racing. Here, Dodge driver Marvin Panch takes on a '56 Ford in his no 98 D-500.

along with two other factory drivers, set no less than 307 records at the Bonneville Endurance Trials in 1956 D-500s. This AAA 14 day continuous trial covered endurance, performance and speed records. The D-500s set more records there than all the other manufacturers attending put together!

Not content with just the AAA wins, Danny Eames also took top honors at NASCAR's Daytona Speed Trials when he won his class (#6 new, 305-350in^3) with a record run of 130.577mph for the 'two-way flying mile'. This run even beat four Chrysler 300Bs that ran in class #7 (new, over 350in^3). Eames also won the Mechanix Illustrated acceleration run championship, again beating a 300B, to become Acceleration Champion of 1956. Wins at NASCAR, USAC and IMCA circuits were many, but the D-500 made an even bigger impression on the drag strip. Edward Lyons of Grayville, Illinois campaigned a D-500-1 and went undefeated in Factory Stock, Super Stock, Super Stock Modified and 'C' gas classes. Ed never lost a single race in the 1956 season. This winning alliance between Ed Lyons and his '56 Dodge culminated in him taking the Super Stock Trophy and Factory Super

Drag strip king. While the '56 Dodges were taking the racetrack by storm, more records were being broken by the D-500s on the strip. Edward Lyons of Grayville, Illinois, campaigned a D-500-1 throughout 1956 and went undefeated in Factory Stock, Super Stock, Super Stock Modified and 'C' gas classes. (The choice of class depended on the officials' placement of the D-500-1 in competition.) The crowning glory was Ed's victory in the Super Stock Trophy followed by his win in the Super Stock Eliminator with a record-breaking run of 102.389mph at the third World Series held at Lawrenceville, Illinois, in August 1956. Sanctioned by the Automobile Timing Association of America (ATAA), this run took Ed Lyons into the history books as driver of the first ever stock American production car to break the 100mph mark over the ¼ mile. This rare shot shows Lyons leaving a Studebaker at the line: believe it or not, Ed used to pull away in second gear!

Ed Lyons outside his home in Grayville, Illinois, with his record-breaking factory D-500-1 and a hood-full of trophies, including one for the Super Stock Eliminator win.

Stock Eliminator. This, with a record breaking run of 102.389mph which holds the distinction of being the first stock American production car to exceed 100mph in the ¼ mile.

It is worth mentioning here that Dodge also took away Ford's monopoly in the law enforcement market, when it produced ChryCo's first ever 'Police Package' in 1956. The Pursuit 230 was an all-rounder squad car. Based on the D-500 model, it had an extra-heavy-duty chassis, electrics, transmission, suspension, brakes, and an engine option list that would make drag racers green with envy. The 230 came from the 230bhp produced by the standard Pursuit 315in³ V8 engine. The California Highway Patrol ordered 600 alone (400 polysphere 315in³ motors and 200 with the Hemi-head). But it wasn't all speed. Its main appeal was dependability – a car that was comfortable, could idle for hours, cruise economically at low speeds and have fast acceleration along with being used almost 24 hours a day, 365 days a year. The '56 Dodge couldn't be beaten and started an illustrious relationship with police forces all over the US (along with Plymouth in 1957 and Chrysler in 1961 with its Enforcer), which lasted well in to the eighties.

(Right) This advert from August 1956 was just one of a host put out by Dodge division, underlining the exclusivity of the D-500. The D-500 model was being watered-down as option packages across the Dodge range were released. The following year it was only an option and no longer a model.

This "Baby" Takes 'em all!

One second you're idling at the light, the next you're off like a flash—out ahead of the pack with nothing in front but the wide open road!

For this is the fabulous Dodge D-500—the car that whipped *all other cars* in acceleration at Daytona Beach and is racking up victory after victory on tracks all over the country.

Here, in a standard production car, Dodge now gives you the red-hot performance you could only get in an expensive custom job.

This baby digs out like a demon, handles like a dream, corners like a chopped-down "rod" with a load of sand. It features a hefty 260 hp. mill and giant 12-inch center-plane brakes.

What's more, the D-500 is available in *all models*, sold and serviced at any Dodge dealership in America. And it's yours for only slightly more than $100.00 over regular Dodge models.

So drive a D-500 soon. You'll understand why *guys who really know cars call it the hottest thing on wheels!*

America's Acceleration Champion

260 hp. aircraft-type V-8 with 315 cubic inch displacement. 9.25 to 1 compression ratio. Bore 3.63 inches, stroke 3.80 inches. Also: 12-inch center-plane brakes with 15½ lbs. of car weight per sq. in. of lining area—a figure unequalled in American passenger cars—and one that approaches most sports cars and even racing cars.

FREE! Illustrated D-500 Brochure.
Write: Advertising Dept., DODGE DIVISION, Detroit 31, Michigan

Dodge D-500

KEEP YOUR EYE ON THE D-500...IT'S A REAL BOMB!

Beautifully poised, this is how Virgil Exner's second generation 'Forward Look' was styled for Dodge. Of all the ChryCo cars, Dodge without doubt had the most fussy appearance, with more use of brightwork than the others; but for 1957, at least, it worked. Longer by 6½ inches, lower and wider, these cars wowed the public and Dodge sales soared. The car shown here is a Coronet Lancer convertible, which was on offer for the first time that year. This was the cheapest choice for racers wanting to enter a Dodge in the NASCAR Convertible Class, and with a price tag of just $2842 it was a hit with the public, too.

THE FORWARD LOOK

The success story of the 1956 D-500 carried on to 1957, but had now sadly been relegated to just an optional performance package and not a series. Standard V8s for the '57 range were the 325in³ Red Ram V8 with polyspherical heads which gave 245bhp, and the Super Red Ram which came as standard on the Custom Royal series and offered 285hp. The D-500 option was available on any Dodge at extra cost, and the same 325in³ mill but with the Hemi-head would give 310hp. The D-501 (for racing only) once again used a Hemi but this time it was on the 354in³ Chrysler engine as used in the 300Bs.

With the introduction of Virgil Exner's second generation of the 'Forward Look', the all-new '57 models received torsion bar suspension along with their rakish new looks. This mechanical advancement alone, which replaced the front coil springs and shock absorbers, made the cars far more agile and comparable to much

Dick Joslin in his no 71 Dodge two-door hardtop is seen here cornering with a '57 Chevy, driven by Bob Welborn. The years 1957-59 were quiet for the division, with no NASCAR wins to its credit until Jim Cook drove to victory in September 1960 at Sacramento.

1958 Custom Royal Lancer D-500. Sticking to a winning formula, the Dodge for 1958 was a mild facelift of the 1957 swept-wing style, concentrating mainly on the front grille. This Custom Royal Lancer D-500 was the sportiest of the bunch.

smaller European sports cars in their handling. The fins that had started off as small chrome appendages back in 1954 were now almost fully grown, and climbed from their start point halfway down the car, to a chrome-tipped peak just above the rear light cluster. Public response to the new 'swept-wing' styling was positive, and sales rose enough to push Dodge up from 8th place to 7th in the manufacturers ratings – but the sales success was short lived. Due to the high demand for the '57 models, Dodge, along with other Corporation cars, let quality control go unchecked. Early rust-out (seen at its worst on Plymouth vehicles), along with squeaks and knocks from poor fit and finish, cost Chrysler Corporation dearly. Going in to a recession in 1958 didn't help, either. Quality was improved as time passed, but the damage was done and the spectre of metal corrosion haunted Chrysler for many years after. Sales for 1958 plummeted to a decade low of just 133,953 for

the model year, against the previous years total of 281,359.

If production was down for 1958, power output was definitely not. Although the old L-head six would see only one more year of production it was still hanging in there with a rating of 138bhp from the 230in^3, but there was an array of V8s to choose from which most buyers went for. The expensive Hemi was dropped from production that year (and not seen again until its reincarnation in the sixties), to be replaced by the wedge head, a single rocker design that was far cheaper to build and would prove reliable and potent.

The smallest version was the Red Ram. This base V8 had a cubic displacement of 325in and let out an impressive 245bhp at 4400rpm, using a 2-barrel Stromberg carburettor (Coronet models). Next came the Super Red Ram, another 325in^3 mill that gave 265hp at 4600rpm and used a Carter 2-barrel (Royal models). If you wanted a little more power for your dollar, how about the Ram Fire

V8? This 350in^3 motor gave 295bhp at 4600rpm. The next step up was the 361in^3 wedge known as the D-500. This was an option now on all Dodges, so even the most mundane Coronet could turn into a 'street sleeper'. With a single 4-barrel carb setup, you could make the most of the 305 horsepower on tap to leave the competition at the lights on Main Street.

A Super D-500 was another alternative, and using two 4-barrel carbs you could expect to get 320bhp. Optioned that year on the Super D-500 was a Bendix fuel injection system that would boost your horsepower up to an incredible 333 horses. Twelve cars were fitted with this very high-performance option, but unfortunately the Bendix FIS proved to be so troublesome that it was removed from all twelve cars shortly after and reverted back to the 2x4 system.

It may seem incredible today to think of such a selection of engines being available, but Dodge was not unusual. All the top manufacturers

at this time were pampering to the power needs of the public as the performance war intensified.

So although Dodge had no single performance car now to match Plymouth's Fury or Chrysler's 300 letter series cars, because of their lightweight nature, *all* Dodges were potential racers. This continued into the early sixties, with the D-500 staying as a performance option for the speed-orientated buyer.

When Kiekhaefer retired from racing, Chrysler was left with no large team to sponsor, only individuals. Kiekhaefer's drivers went to other makers – Fonty Flock went to Mercury, Buck Baker went to Chevy, etc. Lee Petty, an independent, left the arms of Mother Mopar for Oldsmobile, although he was tempted back to Plymouth midway through the '59 season. So racing took a back seat for ChryCo with

no Grand National wins at all for Chrysler, Plymouth or Dodge in the 1958 season, and no wins for Dodge in 1959 either. Up against Ford's new 312in³ motor, Old's J2 Rocket, and the new small block Chevy, the competition was stiff.

Politics was now playing a bigger part in motor racing. Many people were not happy with the major involvement and money that Ford and GM were plowing in, creating what was perceived as a monopoly, but at the same time, these two companies were not happy with the sales returns on this huge investment. In 1957, the Automobile Manufacturers Association (which Ford and GM had joined) outvoted the two big makers and agreed to pull out of motorsport sponsorship, forcing GM and Ford to do likewise. The end result of this was generally good news, not bad. It meant that smaller teams or

1959, head on. Subtle it wasn't, but Dodge's second facelift of the '57 Forward Look had its admirers. The longest, lowest and widest of the late '50s finned cars, it was also the most chrome encrusted. Staying on the previous year's 122in wheelbase, the overall length grew to 217.4 in. The fins also grew to new heights, and the headlamp surrounds became drooping chrome eyebrows. The biggest news was the introduction of the new 383in³ V8, which was available as the D-500 option with a single 4-barrel carb and gave 320bhp, or 345 with dual 4-barrel carbs.

independent drivers now had a fairer chance to win races, but still with the performance equipment that the major manufacturers continued to build. And this 'factory ban' seemed to have little or no effect on the growth of stock car or drag racing as it continued to grow in popularity. FoMoCo (Ford) and GM still took a big interest in racing but via the back door.

Marvin Panch and the 1962 Dart. This was the mount of choice for Mopar racers in 1962 – the Dodge Dart or its lighter Plymouth stable mate, the Belvedere. Although severely stunted in the styling department, when fitted with the Ramcharger engine it was a force to be reckoned with, and was tested by Car Life magazine as one of the top five performance cars of 1962. However, success at the oval track turned out to be elusive for ChryCo drivers this season. The 1961 Daytona 500 winner, Marvin Panch, drove a Dart for the 1962 season but failed to repeat his success of the previous year in his 1961 Pontiac. Ironically, it was Pontiac that swept the board in NASCAR and took the manufacturers' title, with Panch's ex-team-mate Joe Weatherlcy taking the drivers' championship.

The all-new Dart advertising for 1960 was aimed directly at rebuilding public confidence in the marque. This picture, taken from a brochure, tells of the 'fortress of steel' uni-body shell, that is 'Stronger, Spacious, Silent and Rustproofed'. Gone was the separate body on chassis.

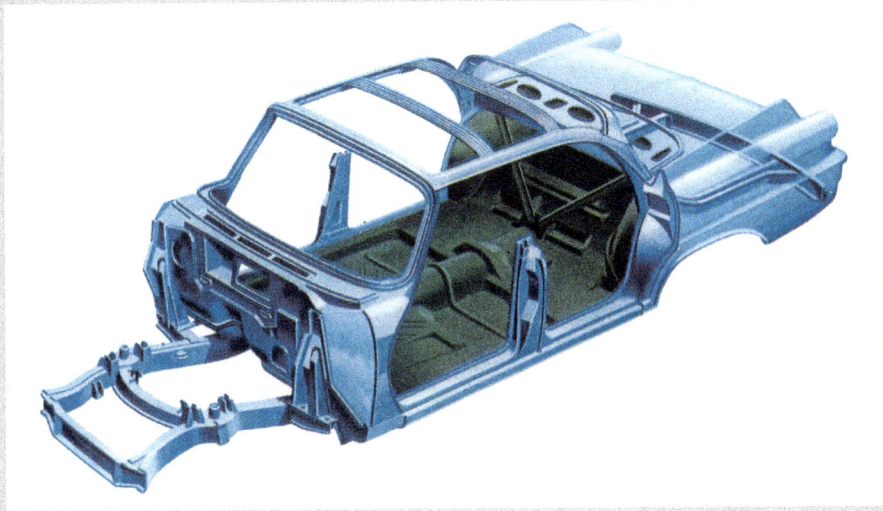

We'll call them the quiet years, but it is all relative, of course. During this period, Dodge never ceased to build performance cars and racers never ceased to drive them, but it was later in the decade that Dodge (and Plymouth) would make a bigger splash in the performance game. For the new decade, Dodge, along with all other divisions, had an all-new car. Except for Imperial, all divisions adopted 'uni-body' construction in 1960. Out went the old 'body bolted on to chassis', and in came an all-welded, one-piece body that had integral strengthening with no bolts or joints to rattle or squeak.

This new construction idea worked well and became a Corporation trademark, but didn't help Chrysler in the fight against rust. Styling had also run amok. When Exner stole the styling leadership in the mid-fifties, the whole Corporation shared a similar theme or design, which was then interpreted to suit the different marques, giving an identifiable corporate 'look' across the board – but now the divisions were drifting apart. Chrysler Division built on the styling cues of its '59 models. Plymouth went overboard with huge fins (as did Imperial) and a scalloped front end, DeSoto, now

This unusual picture shows a pre-production model of the new small Dodge Dart 1960 series. The car shown is one of the flagships of the line, a Phoenix four-door, pillarless hardtop. Phoenix was the top trim level above the base Seneca and medium trim Dart Pioneer. Introduced to complement the full-size Polara and Matador models, its lighter weight lent itself to drag racing and the car enjoyed considerable success at local meets throughout America. The base engine for the Phoenix was an in-line six with V8 options ranging from a mild 230bhp 318 through 361in³ mills up to a 383in³ motor with a new Ram induction setup that gave 330bhp.

METAL PREPARATION, FORMING & FABRICATION OPERATIONS

Cleaning | Drawing Compound | Shear

Cleaning and Coating with Drawing Compound ➡ Drawing & Forming ➡ Body Parts ➡ Body Assembly

6 SPRAY OPERATIONS – EXTERNAL ONLY

| Alkaline Cleaning 170°-180° | 1st Water Rinse 150°-160° | 2nd Water Rinse 140°-150° | Phosphate Coating 125°-135° | Cold Water Rinse | Conditioner Rinse 140°-150° |

7 IMMERSIONS – EXTERNAL & INTERNAL

| Alkaline Cleaning 170°-180° | 1st Water Rinse 150°-160° | 2nd Water Rinse 140°-150° | Phosphate Coating 125°-135° | Cold Water Rinse | Conditioner Rinse 140°-150° | Rust Preventive Primer Coating | Oven Dry |

9 EXTERNAL & INTERNAL FINISHING OPERATIONS

Sill

| 1st Coat Exterior with Epoxy Primer | Coat Sills Inside with Epoxy Primer | 2nd Coat Exterior with Epoxy Primer | Oven Bake 350°-370° | Wet Sanding Exterior | 1st Coat Exterior Lustre Bond Enamel | Coat Sills Inside with Wax | 2nd Coat Exterior Lustre Bond Enamel | Oven Bake 250° |

CHRYSLER CORPORATION'S UNIBODY CORROSION PROTECTION

in it's final death throes, became a Chrysler twin, and the bizarre-looking Valiant, adopted by Plymouth in '61, debuted. Incredibly, it was Dodge, known to some for its garish excess, which faired better than the rest. After a poor sales year in 1959, Dodge hit back with some handsome sculptured styling, toned down from the previous year, that had an unusual rendition of the rear fins and a front grill that dipped down in the center. While Plymouth was quickly slipping down the sales ladder, Dodge jumped up to 6th place with sales that bettered any other division.

The biggest news for Dodge in 1960 was the introduction of a new, smaller car. The Dart sold alongside the 'full-size' Polara and Matador models and was available in three trim lines, starting with the base Dart Seneca, then Pioneer and top of the range Dart Phoenix. This was Dodge's introduction to the 'low price three' market, and for the performance enthusiasts, the start of a series that would offer very lightweight bodies with huge power plants. A powerful 145bhp slant six was the base engine, with a choice of no less than five V8s available to

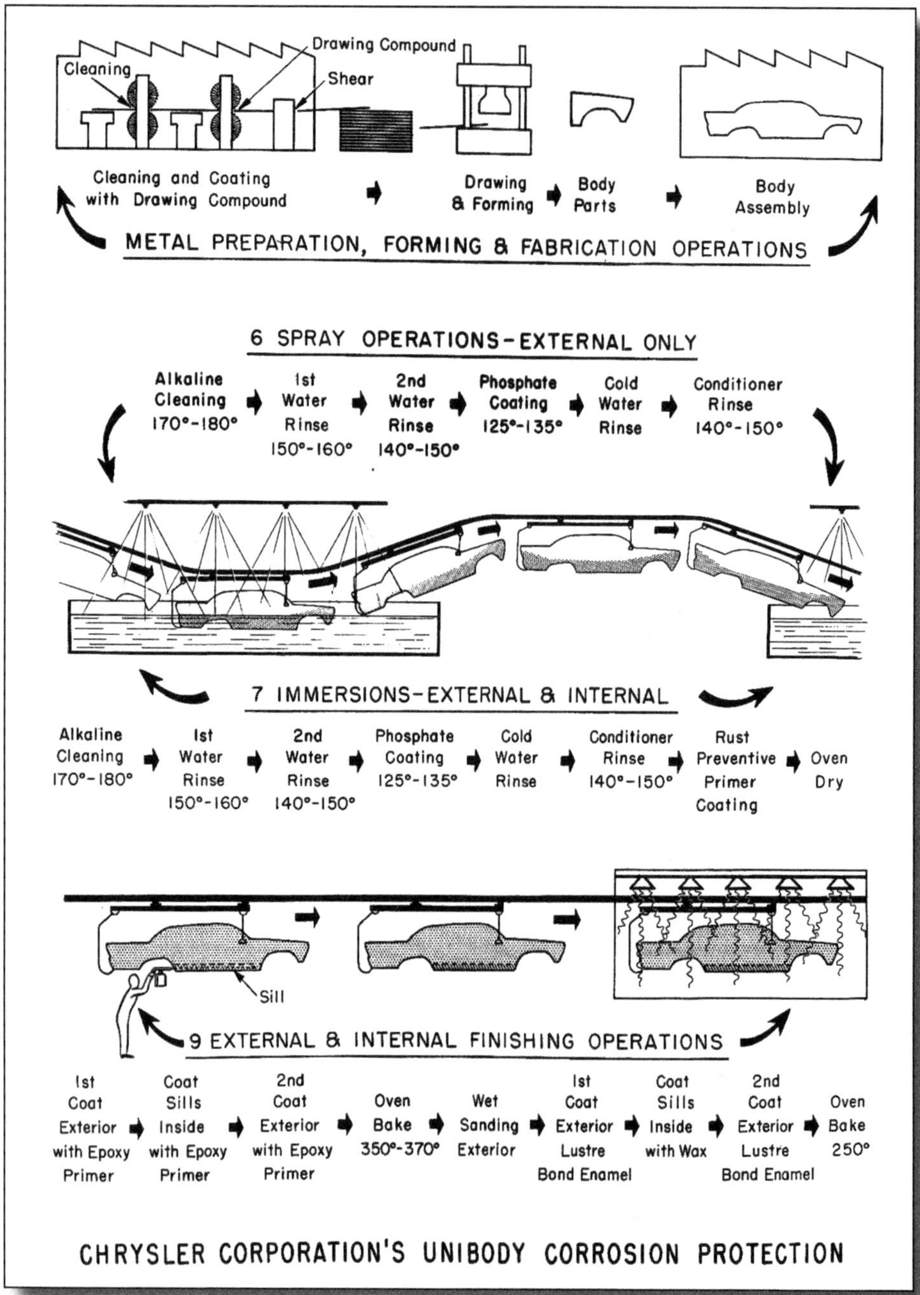

From the horrors of the late 1950s Chrysler learned quickly that early rust-out and poor quality would not be accepted by consumers. In 1960 the company introduced 'uni-body' construction, along with a pre-paint dip to protect the cars. This was all done very much in the public eye and ChryCo even produced this postcard to help get the message across.

1960 Dart – "Sparkling performance with quiet quality". By today's standards this was a large car, but in the early '60s these 208.6in vehicles were the smallest Dodge had to offer. This is the top of the line Phoenix convertible, sitting between the standard 145bhp slant-six and the largest 383in³ D-500 engine.

The new D-500 Ram induction, 383in³ V8 was optional at extra cost on the larger Polara and Matador lines in 1960. The Ram induction principle delivered supercharged performance in mid-speed ranges, increasing torque by as much as 10 per cent. It was with an engine of this type that racer Norm Thatcher reached a speed of 191.8mph in a '60 Dodge.

Again utilizing the 'all-new' construction method, the full-size Dodges had improved handling and build quality, helped by the 'Torsion-Aire' suspension. This 1960 Polara four-door hardtop dripped luxury and extras – swivel seats, central door locks, full-time power steering, new 'Astrophonic' radio, and the 383 or 361 V8.

Norman Thatcher used a 1960 Phoenix to set a new world record at the Bonneville Speed Trials in the B-supercharged gas class with a run of 191.8mph. When Dodge introduced its all new 'intermediate' size car for 1960 it became an instant hit with the drag racing fraternity. Sitting on a 118in wheelbase, the cars were 4in shorter than the full-size Polara and Matador lines and weighed considerably less. Polara two-door hardtop coupes came in at 3740lb compared to just 3410lb for the same body-style Phoenix. The '60 Phoenix in which Norm Thatcher set three new world records had a supercharged 383in³ V8. In 1962, Thatcher set another new record of 167.3mph, this time in Class B production, with a specially prepared Dart fitted with a 413in³ Ramcharger V8.

the Dart Phoenix, culminating with the D-500 option again. This time the big 383in³ motor was used, and could be fitted with the new 'ram induction' setup. Two 4-barrel carbs sat individually on long aluminum intake manifolds that created a supercharger effect and up to 330 horsepower. Even with this equipment, Dodge picked up only one Grand National win at the track that season, and due to Oldsmobile retiring from stock car racing altogether, the Petty family returned to Plymouth and managed to gain eight wins, but Chrysler didn't take a single checkered flag. The new small Dodge seemed to be a match made in heaven for the drag racers though, notching up victories throughout the States. Drag racer Norm Thatcher even set a new record at the Bonneville speed trials, with a run of 191.8mph in a Dart Phoenix.

The following year predictably saw horsepower grow, but also saw the introduction of the Plymouth Valiant-based Dodge Lancer. The public was saying that it wanted smaller automobiles, especially when the recession took hold in 1958. To underline this, cars like the small VW Beetle and other foreign imports were selling well, along with the homegrown Rambler, so Chrysler

announced that it would build its first compact. Ford and GM were slightly ahead of the game already, with work on their Falcon and Corvair well under way. Chrysler bosses still dragged their collective corporate feet until it was obvious even to them that a sea change in taste was developing. Exner gave Chrysler another huge success with his Valiant and Lancer design.

Originally called the Falcon, after one of Exner's previous 'idea cars', the Valiant was renamed after Ford and Chrysler bosses came to an agreement that gave Ford the Falcon. Exner had wanted to get away from large fins and go for a cleaner, smoother look. The new cars were a hastily modified version of a larger design intended for Plymouth, called the Super Sport. With the decision to downsize, the Super Sport never got past the full-size clay model stage, but most of its styling cues went directly into the new compact design. The cars, built at the Dodge plant in St Louis, Missouri, were all four-door sedans and featured typical Exner touches inspired by European styles: the radiator-sized front grille, radiused wheelarches, sports deck trunk lid, and classic long nose and short rear deck proportions. Exner

wanted to see a continuous curve from the roof down to the sills, which required thinner doors and almost flush window-to-door fitting. Odd-looking in this shrunken version perhaps, but they were incredibly successful, priced between the Falcon and Corvair. Out of the three, the Valiant (and then Lancer) was the best engineered, the best handling and the quickest. The Valiant debuted in 1960, interestingly as a marque of its own, and it wasn't until 1961 that it became a Plymouth Valiant or Dodge Lancer in America (although it became a Chrysler around the world, except for Canada, where it remained its own marque).

The 1961 Lancer came in two lines, the base Lancer 170 and a higher spec Lancer 770. The rest of the Dodge line-up faired little better in the styling stakes, the low point being the strange fins that started large and tailed off towards the rear of the car. The public agreed and sales plummeted, pushing Dodge back to 9th position.

The little Dodges may have been plum ugly but they could still shift. Standard on the Lancer was the cast iron slant six, which had actually dropped some cubes and was down to 170in³ from last year's

The restyled Dart for 1961 was not a big hit with the public. A new concave grille under a fairly flat hood was not very flattering, but the strange fins that started high and got lower near the back of the car were disliked even more. Not surprisingly, sales dropped.

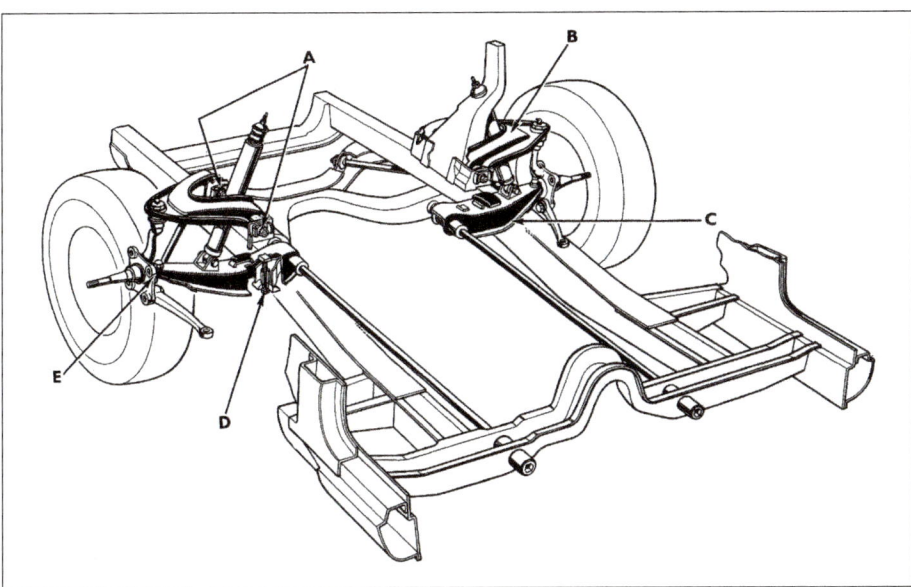

Torsion-Aire suspension, 1961. First introduced on the 1957 model cars, Dodge's Torsion-Aire ride used torsion bar suspension with Oriflow shocks to replace front coil springs. The supple torsion bars absorb the dips and bounces in the road, giving a much smoother and more controlled ride. This was no gimmick. It worked very well indeed and would be found on ChryCo cars for decades.

225in³ displacement, but as an option you could pay $403 more and get a dealer-fitted power pack. This was either the new aluminum block (available later in the model year) or the iron block slant six with a performance setup called a 'Hyper-pak'. Designed purely for competition use, it consisted of the 225in³ block, a more radical cam, high compression pistons, and a Carter 4-barrel carb sitting on top of an intake manifold, which featured long ram passages and steel tubing exhaust headers that ran down to a specially tuned large bore exhaust system.

All this gave an official output of 195bhp, but unofficially it was rated at over 275bhp – more power than

Dodge's standard 318 or 361 V8s could offer – and again, it was at the drag strip that these cars would rule the lower stock classes.

For the larger Dodge lines, the new 413 V8 appeared for the first time this year within the D-500 options. Either the 350hp Super D-500 or the Super Ram Induction D-500 V8, which gave an extra 25 horsepower, were available as an option on the full-size Polara only (the Matador series lasted just one year).

I say the 'new' 413, but it wasn't strictly new. It was the bored-out 383, but for 1962 the 413in³ 'Max Wedge'

POLARA CONVERTIBLE V8

1961 Polara D-500 convertible. This was Dodge's highest offering, the convertible version of its 'custom-sized' Polara series. Billed as the "finest of everything Dodge" it featured a restyled tail-end with large torpedo-tube type lights and the controversial reverse-slant fins. Power came from a 325bhp 383in³ V8 although another 5hp could be gained from the optional cross-Ram induction setup.

was released. Based on the 'Raised Block' (RB) engine, Dodge shared this mill with Plymouth. Dodge named its the Ramcharger (in deference to Dodge's drag strip team) and Plymouth dubbed its simply Super Stock.

The motor had larger porting and bigger valves, forged steel crank and connecting rods, lightweight alloy

INTRODUCING THE FANTASTIC POLARA 500. You have never driven an automobile like this one. It is definitely not for the casual driver. This limited-production 1962 Dodge is powered by a lusty 361 cubic inch V8 with four-barrel carburetion, a high-performance cam, and dual exhausts. The interior is magnificent. Saddle-grained vinyl upholstery. Individually adjustable bucket seats. Courtesy console. Sill-to-sill carpeting. The car is available as a convertible (shown above) or in a hardtop series. One more point. The 1962 Dodge Polara 500 is a very special automobile. Do not expect everybody to own one. COME IN AND DRIVE THE NEW LEAN BREED OF DODGE.

pistons, twin Carter AFB carbs (again sitting on ram intakes that had 15in individual runners), a choice of two compression ratios (11.0:1 or 13.5:1), and large diameter free-flowing exhaust manifolds and pipes. All this was married to either a heavy-duty 3-speed manual box with a floor shift, or to the new H-D Torqueflite 3-speed automatic with dash-mounted push buttons. The thing was almost bullet proof, and at the drag strip it started to turn heads. In July of '62 Tommy Grove used a Max Wedge-powered Plymouth to clock the first ever

1962 Polara 500 advert. Polara was now a medium-size car aimed at the luxury sports car market. Initially it was only available as a two-door hardtop or a convertible (shown here), but a four-door hardtop was later released. The Polara 500 was powered by a standard 265bhp 361 V8 with an optional power boost of 305bhp. Standard features included bucket seats, full carpeting, dual exhausts, reversing light and cigar lighter.

sub-12 second run in a 'stocker', but on the racetrack it still couldn't quite match the competition. ChryCo wasn't the only camp with a powerful wedge engine, as Pontiac drivers had the hottest wheels that year in their 421in³-powered Catalinas, and even Chevy's famous 409 was proving hard to beat. Time for some minor adjustments!

MORE LIVE ACTION-LESS DEAD WEIGHT. The full-size '62 Dodge Dart will accelerate seven percent quicker than last year's comparable model, and do it on five percent less gas. Main reason? Dead weight has been cut to a minimum. For instance, the automatic transmission housing, for V8s, used to be made of cast iron, now it's aluminum. The new one is stronger, and 60 pounds lighter. If you're looking for a low price car with a fistful of action, you have found it. COME IN AND DRIVE THE NEW LEAN BREED OF DODGE.

1962 Dart 440 advert. Stylistically challenged, but very fast – that was the new 1962 Dart. This advertisement declares the 440 to be the "first of the action-economy cars", with "more live action – less dead weight". Some 86,885 V8-powered Darts were sold in 1962, but this figure was still down on the previous year's total of 100,500 and nowhere near 1960's high of 187,000.

1962 Dart 440. The 440 was the top trim level for the Dart intermediate-size series, going down through the 330 series to the basic Dart. These models were 10in shorter than the '61 Darts and considerably lighter, which meant they were picked for racing. For power, the top engine was the new 'Max Wedge' Ramcharger 413 V8 that could give up to 420bhp. Here, the four-door sedan is being put through its paces at Chrysler's proving grounds.

1962

The power war was just about to escalate once more, and Dodge was going to lead from the front. But for Dodge dealerships and potential Dodge buyers, the early sixties was a confusing time. Downsizing was all the rage and body changes were hard to keep up with. As mentioned, the full-sized Matador was only seen for one year (1960), leaving the Polara as the flagship in '61, positioned above the slightly shorter Dart Seneca, Pioneer and Phoenix, with the compact Lancer 170 and 770 at the bottom of the heap. However, for 1962 the Polara was shrunk in size, in the mistaken belief that this was what GM intended for its full-size Chevrolet models. When it became clear that this was not the case, the larger Custom 880 series was introduced mid-year to fill out the range – a car which was based on the Chrysler Newport.

1962 Lancer. The smallest Dodge available was the compact Lancer. Based on Plymouth's Valiant, it shared almost everything except front clip and trim. The car shown, a Lancer GT, is actually a show car featuring a sliding fabric roof made by Golde Body Parts. It did the autoshow circuits but the idea never went into production. The 170bhp slant-six-powered Lancer series was dropped entirely in 1963.

Vigil Exner's stylish design for the ill-fated Plymouth Super Sport really was much more apparent in the cars of '62. The larger Polara and Custom models (along with Plymouth's Sport Fury) arguably wore the European style better than the smaller cars. Exner wasn't happy with these any of these cars, due mostly to the overwhelming compromises he had to make to get the design to work on ever-shrinking wheelbases. The public agreed and sales continued to slip to a decade low of 240,484 units.

Numbers were 'in' for '62, so the Polara became the Polara 500

1962 Lancer interior. This was the luxury interior of the 1962 Lancer Gran Turismo, Dodge's new compact sports model. It featured front bucket seats and shimmering all-vinyl upholstery. Rear seats were bucket-type with pleated inserts. Power accessories were no problem: power brakes, seats and steering were all available, along with an electric clock, air-conditioning and a Music Master radio.

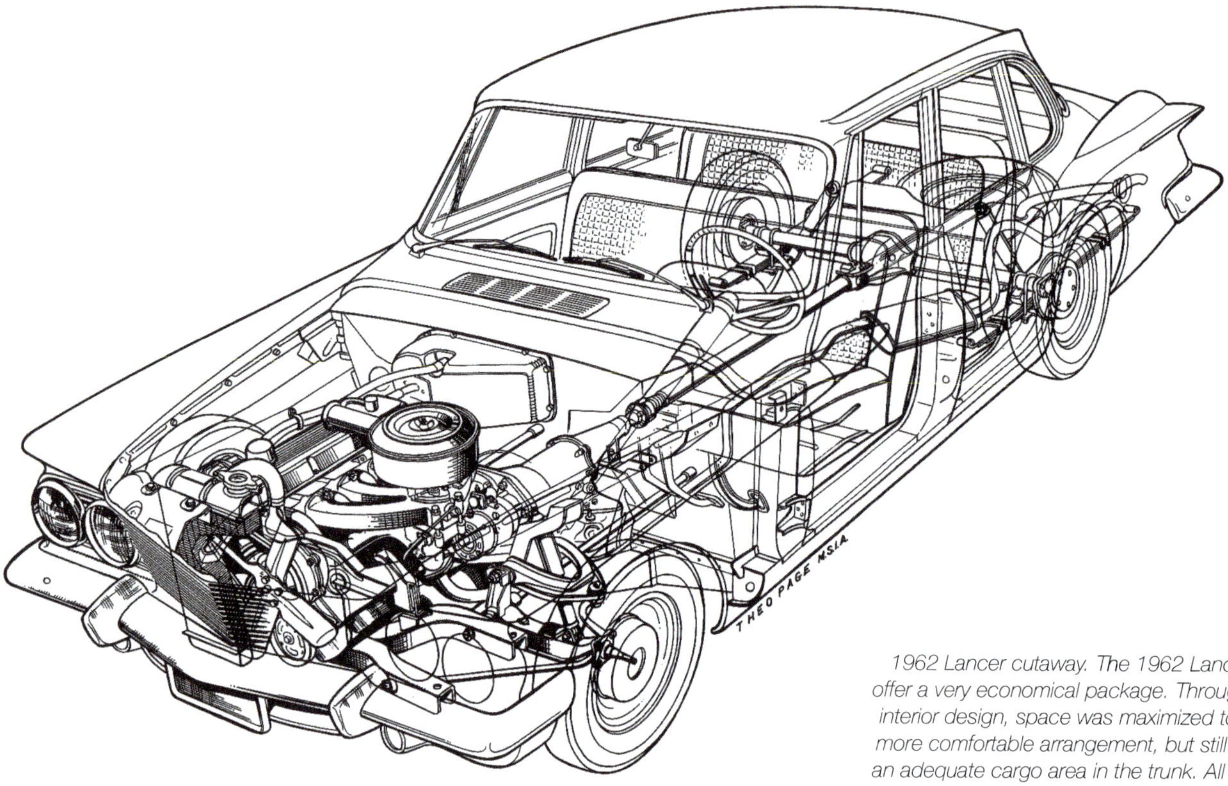

1962 Lancer cutaway. The 1962 Lancer did offer a very economical package. Through good interior design, space was maximized to give a more comfortable arrangement, but still provide an adequate cargo area in the trunk. All Lancers were powered by slant-six engines.

series in the medium price and size bracket. The Dart also shrunk, almost down to the size of the compact Lancers, but what they lost in styling and length, they made up for in numbers. The base trim level was simply Dart, then came the Dart 330 and Dart 440. The Lancers, now in their final year, were still numbered 170 and 770 but saw a new top of the range line come in called the Gran Turismo (GT).

The following year things got a little simpler. The full-size Custom 880 had a facelift and remained the flagship for Dodge. The standard size offerings consisted of the Polara, Dodge 330 and Dodge 440, and because the Lancer had been dropped completely, a new, slightly larger compact was introduced and took on the Dart name. The three series lines were the entry-level 170, medium 270 and top trim GT. Phew!

As styling got boxier and car sizes got progressively smaller, engines became increasingly powerful. The ban on manufacturers' involvement in motorsports was falling apart, as Ford and GM wholeheartedly got back in to full team sponsorship and started engineering programs designed purely to keep their cars in front on the oval tracks. Ford in particular released a full-scale racing program for 1963 that backed just about anything that

In an effort to boost flagging sales Dodge adopted a new look for 1963. The longer, lower, sleeker lines seem very boxy by today's standards but gave a more modern look back then. The standard-size (intermediate) cars were offered in three series – the base 330, medium trim level 440 and top range Polara. The 330 shown here came equipped with a 225in^3 slant-six but the base V8 was the 230bhp 318. Optional at extra cost were the 383, 413 and new 426in^3 motors.

When the 1963 models were released the small Lancer had been replaced by the now downsized Dart range. The medium or standard-sized Dodge was the 330/440/Polara model with the full-size 880 and Custom 880s at the top. Two production lines worked side-by-side at the Detroit Dodge plant. In the foreground are the compact Darts and in the background the slightly larger Polara models, passing the inspection area at the end of the line.

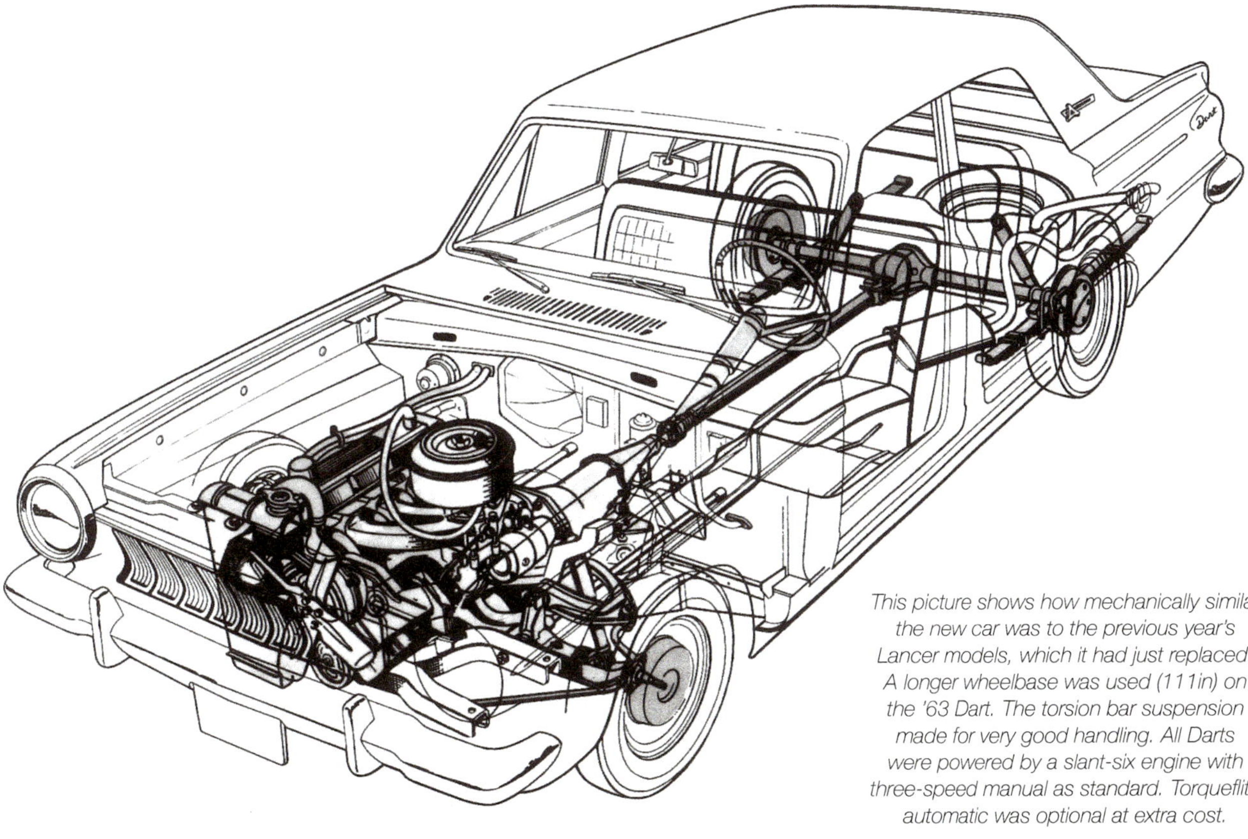

This picture shows how mechanically similar the new car was to the previous year's Lancer models, which it had just replaced. A longer wheelbase was used (111in) on the '63 Dart. The torsion bar suspension made for very good handling. All Darts were powered by a slant-six engine with three-speed manual as standard. Torqueflite automatic was optional at extra cost.

1963 426 Ramcharger engine. The Max Wedge engine introduced in 1962 had now been bored out to 426in³ and was dubbed the Ramcharger II in deference to the Dodge-backed Ramchargers drag team. On the track, this Ram inducted motor wasn't quite a match for the new Ford 427in³ power plant, or even the previous year's 421 wedge Pontiac engine. Although Plymouth managed to find nineteen victories, Dodge didn't make it to the winner's circle once. At the drag strip, however, Herman Mozer (pictured) took a Ramcharger Dodge fitted with the 426–A to the finals of Super Stock and beat another 426in³-powered Ramcharger team car to take the US Nationals championship. He also won Stock Eliminator.

raced on four wheels – Indy, drags, and of course stock car racing. With the exception of Indy racing, Chrysler set about the same goal. Dodge hadn't seen the inside of the winners circle since 1960, and wouldn't see it in the '63 season either. Plymouth faired better, but Mopar fans didn't have much longer to wait. In the fight to beat Pontiac, Chrysler engineers bored the big block engine out to 426in³ and increased the horsepower to 425.

This became the Max Wedge II, or Stage II, and found itself under

the hoods of Dodge cars as the Ramcharger II. It was hoped that this would be enough power to get back in the winning habit again. Unfortunately for Chrysler, it wasn't, because both Chevy and Ford unveiled their big block 427s for the '63 season, with Ford fitting its new engine in the more streamlined new Galaxies. Both of these motors could put out over 425hp. Ford walked away with the '63 championship, winning 23 Grand National races. GM did a major U-turn and withdrew from motor sport.

At the drag strip however, it

was a different story. Jim Thornton's Dodge-backed Ramcharger team swept the board at the NHRA (National Hot Rod Association) Nationals at Indianapolis, when two identical Ramcharger Dodges beat all comers and found themselves against each other in the finals of Super Stock. Al 'The Lawman' Eckstrand won the Stock title at Pomona in a 426-powered Plymouth, but at the ChryCo camp, this wasn't enough. Ford had to be beaten on the oval track.

Teammates Billy Wade (no 5) and David Pearson (no 6) at Daytona during the 1963 NASCAR season. All sizes of car were used in an attempt to get a win for ChryCo, and two can be seen here. The large 122in wheelbase 880 at the back is being led by a 119in WB Dodge 330. A smaller Plymouth was also used. The difference in styling is obvious – Pearson's no 6 Dodge is based on the sleek '63 Chrysler Newport, whereas Wade's boxy but

This picture taken in February 1963 shows Dodge team driver David Pearson with his Cotton Owens-prepared, no 6 Dodge 880 before the running of the Daytona 500. At the end of the season, with no wins to the team's name, Dodge drivers weren't smiling anymore. But they wouldn't have to wait long to see inside the winner's circle again.

In 1963, Dodge made a big deal about its performance capabilities. In many of its adverts, it used a race or drag strip car to accentuate the positive. This ad featured a Cotton Owens 426in³-powered Dodge 440. The 440 model sat between the introductory full-size 330 model and the Polara and Polara 500.

A special engineering team, led by William Weertman and Tom Hoover, was set the goal of building a new super performance V8 engine to be used strictly for racing and have it ready in time for the start of the 1964 NASCAR season, the Daytona 500. Keeping to what they knew worked, Weertman's team married the 426in^3 wedge mill, with its strong lower end, to the famous hemispherical combustion chambers of the 1950s. When dyno testing started in December of '63 the readings went off the 400bhp scale of the in-house meter, so a general horsepower rating of 425bhp was set for the basic engine. Things were looking up!

News of the new 426 Hemi got out, and at the Daytona qualifier on 7 February, 1964 all eyes were on the Dodge and Plymouth cars as they made their debut.

This fantastic picture shows Dodge driver Dick Landy pulling a wheelie in his 1965 Coronet Hemi-Charger at the Lions Drag Strip in Long Beach, California. He had recently won the A/FX class and Top Stock Eliminator titles at Bakersfield with a best time of 10.26 seconds and a top speed of 138mph. This factory-built Super Stocker had an altered wheelbase and used Dodge Dart spindles, brakes and drums in an effort to keep overall weight to a minimum.

Paul Goldsmith, driving a Ray Nichels prepared Belvedere, smashed the previous lap record of 160.943mph with a fastest lap time of 174.910mph. Richard Petty, Lee's son, came close to matching that with a qualifying time of 174.418mph.

The race made motorsport history. From the green flag the Hemi-powered cars led from the front, and when

51

the dust settled at the end of the race, Petty had won and was over a lap ahead of the next car, another Hemi-powered Plymouth. The new 426 Hemi-engineered Dodge and Plymouth cars took four of the top five places and had turned the tables on the all-powerful Fords.

The race following the Daytona was the Richmond 250 and where Dodge took its first win for three seasons, when a Cotton Owens Polara driven by David Pearson took the checkered flag. Two weeks later, he won again at Greenville, South Carolina. The season went on in that fashion, with either the lighter Plymouth or Dodge driving in to the winners circle. Dodge made a total of 14 wins. On the USAC circuit, the story was the same, and at the Firecracker 400, held again at Daytona, a Dodge Polara won the race, followed quickly by five other Hemi-powered cars. By the end of the NASCAR season, ChryCo cars had taken 26 Grand National wins.

1964 Firecracker 400 advert. The premise of "winning on Sunday – selling on Monday" was very prominent with this full-page advert placed in American news journals by Chrysler. The picture shows A J Foyt winning the Firecracker 400 at Daytona in his #47 1964 Polara, swiftly followed by five other 426 Hemi-powered Dodge and Plymouth cars. In fact, seven of the top eight cars were Mopar.

HEMI GETS BANNED

Although the 1964 race season was a tremendous success, storm clouds were on the horizon for the ChryCo camp. As the Dodge and Plymouth cars chalked up more wins, the complaints from the Ford camp grew louder. NASCAR rules stipulated that engines used in race cars had to be production engines available to the public. Chrysler had flagrantly disregarded this. The competition 426 Hemi was only made accessible to a favored few teams and individuals.

In reply, Ford retaliated with the news it was working on its own Hemi-head for the 427, which might be a non-regular production engine, too. With complaints coming in from even the heaviest 'right-footers' in the driving fraternity that speeds were getting too high, this all culminated in the rules for the 1965 season banning the proposed Ford Hemi and

4

1964 Dart GT. For Dodge's fiftieth anniversary all three series lines got a makeover. The compact Dart series had the fewest alterations with most of the changes being to the front grille. From concave to convex, the grille section now also carried DODGE in a black painted bar running the width of the grille section. The series badge now sat where DODGE had been spelled out on the '63 models at the front of the hood bulge. The GT was again the top-of-the-range Dart, and for the first time was given a V8. The extra power from the 273in^3 motor was popular with drag racers and the public. The Dart was the division's best-seller in '64.

For Dodge divison's Golden Anniversary most of its cars received only a mild facelift. This period brochure for the standard-size range used modern, trendy artwork to help sell the revised rooflines and large engines to a younger market. The cars were advertised as the 'Dependables'. This car is a Dart GT.

'high-riser' wedge head, along with Mopar's (MoPar stands for Motor-Parts, Chrysler's spares Division, that also produced performance parts) existing 426 Hemi. This was simply devastating news for the Dodge and Plymouth teams. Mopar's racing chief Ronnie Householder released his own statement in reply to this ban, stating that unless time was given to allow for transition to other engines, Chrysler Corporation would withdraw from all NASCAR sanctioned races and would concentrate on USAC, SCCA and NHRA events instead. Which is what it did. The '65 NASCAR season became a farce. Ford won 32 races in a row and track attendance began to drop considerably because of the lack of competition. NASCAR revised (relaxed) the rules three quarters of the way through the calendar, so the Hemis returned with an end of season flourish. David Pearson took Dodge to 3 wins and Petty had 7 for Plymouth. Ford took the rest.

Away from racing, Dodge celebrated its golden anniversary in 1964. The compact Dart GT received its first V8 (also available on other Dart models) in the form of a 273in^3 motor, along with a mild facelift consisting mainly of a fresh convex grill that had a full-width bar in its center with 'DODGE' written in block capitals. These compact cars proved very popular and became this division's best seller in '64.

The Chargers team, 1964. To many observers, the first Funny Cars were the two blown Dodges run by the Chargers team. Campaigned by Jim Johnson and Jimmy Nix, they debuted in the 1964 season, ran supercharged Max Wedge engines using gasoline, and had bodies designed by noted Californian stylist Dean Jeffries. They attended events as 'booked-in' attractions. However, it soon became evident that more radical fuel mixtures and body modifications would be needed for success, so the cars were retired at the end of the season.

The standard size Dodge was still the Polara. Next came the luxurious full-size Custom 880, which again used the Chrysler Newport as a donor car, but so many panel alterations were made it was hardly recognizable as a Newport and was arguably the best-looking Dodge for many years. The production-based Charger concept car did the rounds of auto shows and would be followed up in '65 with a more predictable Charger II show car.

For the 'street-racer', the 426 Max Wedge Ram Charger was available with yet another update. The cylinder heads were opened up even more, a larger set of 4-barrel carbs sat on the crossram, and new heavy-duty cast iron, fully tuned

The biggest news for 1964 was the introduction of the 426in³ Hemi engine. Available in both Dodge and Plymouth race cars, it was unbeatable on the track and strip. Al Eckstrand, a young attorney, campaigned ChryCo cars to great effect throughout the '60s. His 'Lawman' cars ruled the drag strip. He won 'Mr Stock Eliminator' for the 1963 season in a Ramchargers team Dodge and was the first man in NHRA history to use an automatic gearbox to do it. Through the '64 season he used this factory-built 'drag package' 426 Hemi-powered Plymouth to great effect. (Photograph courtesy of Al Eckstrand)

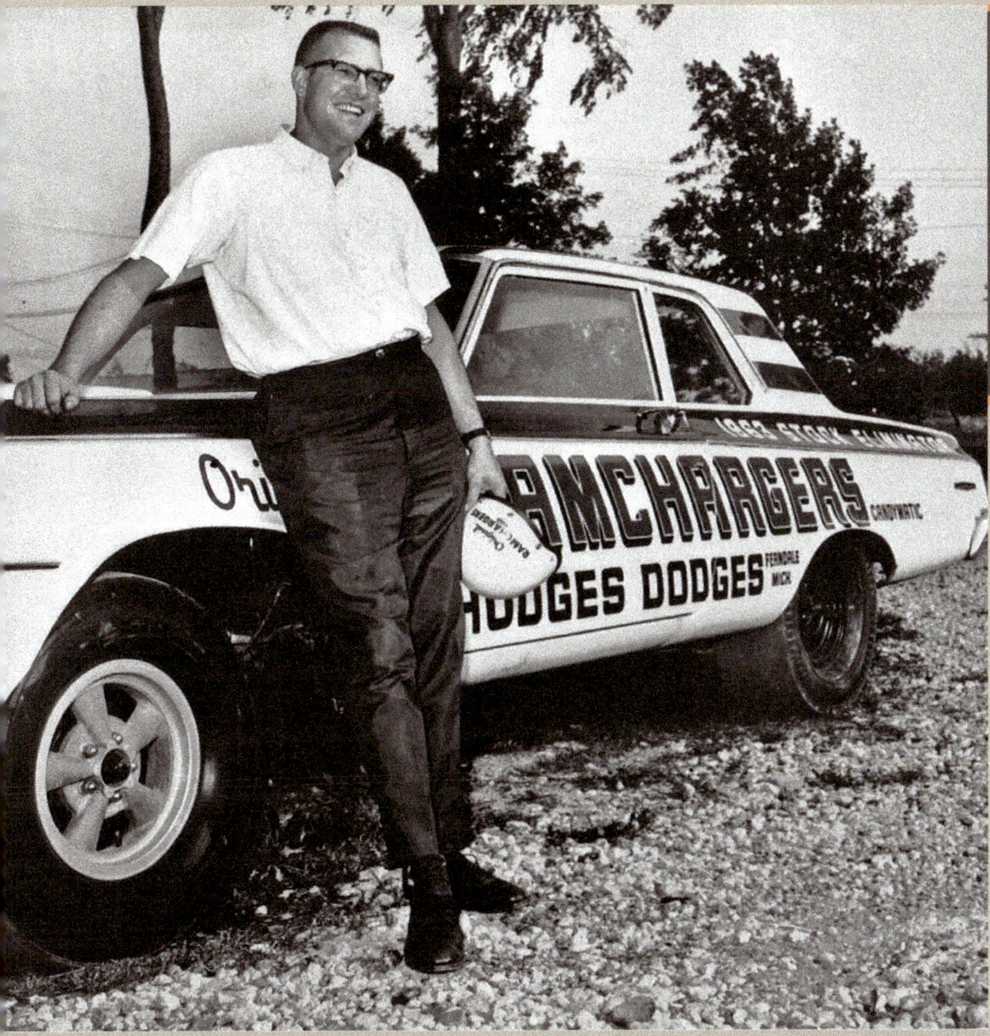

Jim Thornton was the hard-driving President of the Dodge-backed Ramchargers racing team, which worked out of Detroit. He became one of the most competitive stock car drivers in the business, and won the '64 US Nationals. The Ramchargers Maximum Performance Corporation (RMPC) was a group of Chrysler engineers responsible for developing many of the parts and combinations that put ChryCo cars in the winner's circle on race day. The RMPC was set up in 1963 to help promote and sell the performance parts that the engineers had developed outside the factory.

Jim Thornton blasts a Ramcharger Dodge to a new Super Stock Automatic (S/SA) record at the NHRA Summer nationals in 1964, with a run of 11.23 seconds and 130.05mph. The striking red and white striped paint scheme adopted by the Ramchargers team earned the cars the nickname of Candy sticks (for stick-shift cars) and Candy-matics (for auto boxes). The 426 Hemi-powered cars were only allowed to race in the A/FX class initially because of the low numbers of engines available from Dodge. Later in the '64 season the NHRA allowed their use in Super Stock.

exhaust headers were fitted. This became the Stage III setup, and was available on all Dodge cars except the compact Dart lines. At the drag strip, the NHRA deemed the new 426 Hemi to be experimental because of the lack of units, and placed them in the A/FX (A/Factory Experimental) class until part way through the '64 season, before allowing them into Super Stock as availability grew. A factory-built drag package was made in limited numbers and saw Roger Lindamood's 'Color Me Gone' beat another factory Dodge, Jim Thornton's Ramcharger, in the Super Stock finals at Indianapolis. Even FoMoCo's 427 hi-riser powered Comet Cyclones couldn't touch these cars.

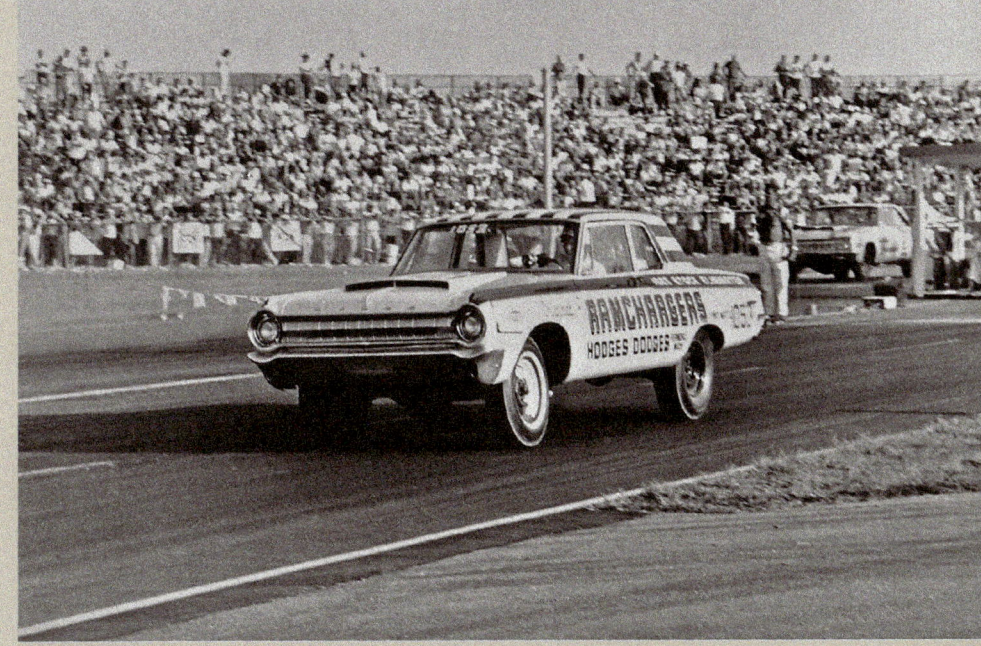

The compact Dodge received an extensive facelift in 1965. New hood, grille, bumpers, trunk lid and lights gave a more aggressive look. Available in three series – Dart, Dart 270 and Dart GT – this is the lavishly equipped GT version. All models came with a standard 101bhp 170in³ slant-six that could be beefed up to 145bhp from a larger 225in³. If that didn't satisfy the performance connoisseur's appetite, a 273in³ V8 was available. When fitted with a Carter four barrel, this could give an impressive 235hp.

For 1965, a new mid-size or intermediate model appeared with the resurrection of the Coronet name, which had been dropped after 1959. Although slightly larger than its Ford Fairlane and Chevy Chevelle rivals, it was smaller than the Polara, which had grown back to being a full-size series, and sitting on a 117in wheelbase, it was 2in shorter than the '64 Polara it replaced. Available as Coronet, Coronet 440 or Coronet 500 (the 330 designation bowed out as a base model number at the end of 1964), this was the series that would prove so successful in the world of motorsport.

The Polara now became the base trim level for the full-size 121in chassis cars. The next trim step up was the Custom 880, now in its final year. Then came a new top range, the Monaco, which was only built in 2-door hardtop form, devised to compete with Pontiac's Grand Prix in the personal luxury sports car market.

The Coronet name made a welcome return to the Dodge line-up for 1965 when an all-new model was introduced. The line featured three series – Coronet, Coronet 440 and Coronet 500. Sitting between the compact Darts and medium-sized Polara lines, it was known as an intermediate-size model. The 117in wheelbase and overall length of just 204.2in gave major weight savings so the car lent itself very well to racing. Base engine was the 225in³ slant-six but it had an array of V8s as extras. The car shown is the base model Coronet four-door sedan.

This cutaway from 1965 shows that torsion-bar front suspension was still very much in favor on ChryCo's full-size cars. This Dodge Polara (and Plymouth Fury) rear suspension comprised semi-elliptical type springs with shock absorbers.

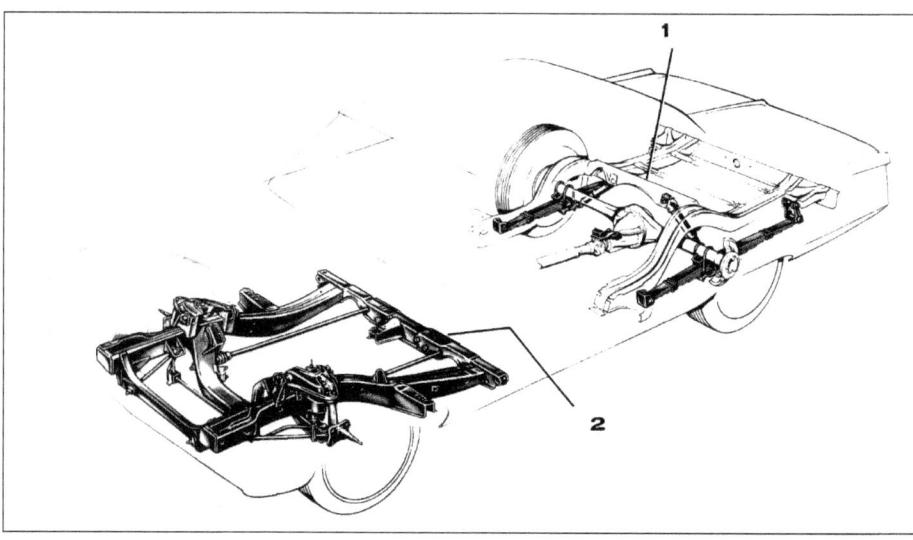

STREET-HEMI DEBUTS

It was never envisaged that the 426 Hemi would be made available to the general public, but pressure from NASCAR rulings set the challenge and Chrysler met it. In 1966, the once pure race engine was made optional on the new Charger fastback, and so the Street Hemi was born. Only slightly de-tuned from its 1964 racing setup, the Street Hemi came

Drag racing legend Bud Faubel campaigned one of the first factory-package drag cars in 1964 with his 'Hemi Honker' Dodge 330, and became the NHRA S/SA champion. Fitted with the 426 race Hemi, Bud's 330 reached the winner's circle on many occasions with regular runs in the low 11 second bracket and speeds of 125mph. For the '65 season, he was back with the new Coronet.

1965 Hemi Honker. The original 1963 Super Stock package included aluminum fenders, hood and scoop, thin steel bumpers, and Plexiglas instead of side glass. But for 1965, fiberglass panels were used extensively on the factory Coronets, including the doors, hood, scoop, trunk lid, and even the bumpers and dash. The interior had just two bucket seats fixed to aluminum runners. These altered-wheelbase cars had the rear wheels moved forward by 15in and the front wheels by 10in, giving greatly improved weight distribution. Power came from the awesome 426in³ Hemi-Charger, which had an official rating of 425bhp but was nearer 550bhp in reality.

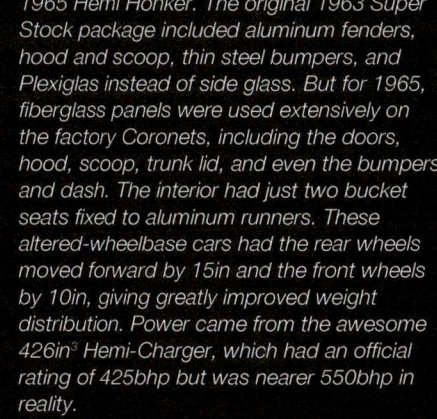

Bobby Harrop was one of a select few who received a factory-altered wheelbase car in 1965. The car was one of the most successful of the season, winning the Super Stock magazine Nationals and barnstorming the eastern United States. The 'Flying Fireman', as he was known, also won the S/SA class at the NHRA Nationals at Indianapolis, with a Hemi Dodge 4090.

A modest facelift for the 1966 Dart predictably concentrated on grille, taillight and trim refinements. Still standard was the 170in³ slant-six with the same 273in³ V8 as in '65, with either the two-barrel 180bhp version or the nippy four-barrel 235bhp. This would be the last year for this type of Dart with a fresh all-new model waiting in the wings, but for '66 this GT convertible was as good as it could get. Dart, Dart 270 and Dart GT were the models, with convertibles available only in the 270 and GT series. All Darts shared the same 111in wheelbase except the smart little station wagon, which could be had in the Dart and 270 series and used a 106in wheelbase.

Although only a year old, the Coronet models came in for a complete re-style in 1966. The Coronet now had a line-up of four models: the base Coronet, the Deluxe, the 400 and this top of the range 500. This was the series that emphasized performance. Riding on a 117in wheelbase, the cars were still medium-size, high-power vehicles with big V8s under the hood. The 500 came standard with a 383 but also available was the biggest engine Dodge ever built, the 440in³ wedge. The 500 came with bucket seats, padded dash, center console, full carpeting and spinner type wheelcovers as standard. The Levant-grain vinyl roof was optional.

1966 Coronet 440. Dodge had a bumper sales year in 1966 with 632,658 units made. This sent the company to fifth place in the ratings and it was the Coronet 440 that sold best. The mix of affordable luxury and power attracted 128,998 buyers. These views of the 440 two-door hardtop show the unusual rear roof quarter styling and the pinched-in waistline that helped to persuade all those customers. Arguably it was one of the best-looking cars of the '60s.

equipped with in-line dual 4-barrel intake and cast iron manifolds instead of the racing cross-ram configuration. This slightly more civilised Hemi was rated at 425bhp at 5600rpm, and was advertised directly at the youth market with an advertising campaign that shouted, "Join the Dodge Rebellion!" All Dodge vehicles had some performance options, with a staggering nine different V8 options available from this division, culminating in the huge 440 wedge and, of course, the Hemi-Charger 'Street Hemi'. Although only a year old, the Coronet series had all-new styling, which saw the car's length shrink by an inch but the width increase slightly. The overall effect was one of being less boxy.

At the track, the tables had been well and truly turned and Mopar drivers cleaned up. Although Ford's 427 SOHC engine had been legalized for NASCAR events, it carried a weight penalty that Ford couldn't agree to, so it was Ford this time that boycotted all NASCAR-sanctioned races from early on in the '66 season. A change in the rules that allowed the use of smaller cars enticed Ford back into the fray late in the season (still without the 427 'Cammer'). It did have some success, but this still didn't stop Dodge driver David Pearson taking the championship with 15 clear wins and 26 top five finishes in his Cotton Owens-prepared Charger.

1966 Polara. The Monaco and the Polara were Dodge's full-size vehicles. Using a 121in wheelbase, all two- and four-door Polaras had an overall length of 213.3in. The boxiest and most conservative of this year's series, the full line-up of nine different models went a long way towards helping the Polara be the second biggest seller for the division with sales of 107,832 units. The base engine was the 318in³ V8 rated at 230bhp, with options on the 270bhp 383 V8 and the new 350bhp 440 wedge.

The dash and instrument panel was unique to the 1966 Charger and again went almost unchanged from the '65 show car. A full-width padded cowl shaded the instruments from sunlight. The instrument panel itself featured four large chrome cowls which held (from left) alternator and fuel gauges, speedometer, tachometer and temperature with oil pressure indicator. This car is fitted with a Torqueflite three-speed auto – the 'T' bar shifter can be seen in the center console. The sporty three-spoke steering wheel was also standard.

The spacious interior of the 1966 Charger was well designed. The two rear bucket seats folded forward, flush with the full-length center console to give a cavernous 7ft-plus of fully carpeted cargo area. The center console itself held courtesy lights at the front, a forward-pivoting section to allow for through access, and stowage areas that doubled as arm rests front and back.

The rear of the 1966 Charger can only be described as massive. The taillights function across the whole width of the car. The cue for this style point, along with many others, came from the 1965 Charger II concept car. The fastback style didn't appeal to everybody. It is one of those cars customers either love or hate, and in 1966 only 37,344 loved it – a figure lower than Dodge anticipated. Compared to Pontiac's GTO sales of over 90,000, it was disappointing. The following year the Charger figures dropped even further to just 15,788.

Mid-way through the 1966 model year, Dodge introduced its fastback Charger. Based very much around the Coronet, it shared the latter's 117in wheelbase, drivetrain, and some body panels, but also had unique features of its own. Quad headlamps hid behind a full-width grille made up of fine vertical convex bars, taillights were also full-width, and inside there were bucket seats front and rear, along with an exclusive instrument panel and a center console housing the floor shift (manual or auto). Under the hood was a 318 V8 as standard, but the Street-Hemi was available on the Charger. Mainly because of the cost (over $700 for this option), only 468 buyers selected this engine.

This 1966 Charger waits in the pit lane for its run down a drag strip some thirty-three years after it was produced. It is fitted with the optional 325bhp 383in³ V8 (four-barrel) matched to a three-speed auto box, and demonstrates the longevity that was built into these fantastic cars. Back in 1966 Dodge driver David Pearson used a similar Charger, fitted with the 426 race-Hemi, to win the NASCAR drivers' championship and helped Dodge take the manufacturers' title.

The very first NASCAR win for a Charger went to Earl Balmer on 25 February at Daytona International Speedway, when he drove the 100 mile (40 lap) qualifying race in a No. 3 Dodge Charger owned by Ray Fox.

The 1967 model year saw more success at the track for Hemi-powered cars. Buddy Baker and new Dodge driver Bobby Allison both took Chargers to the winners' circle, but it was Plymouth's Richard Petty who took the championship title with 27 wins. Drag strip heroes Sox & Martin and Dick Landy returned to drag racing with factory-backed Plymouth Belvederes and Dodge Coronets for Super Stock. The Dodge Rebellion was really heating up. A mild facelift of last year's Coronet and a restyle of the other models using the 'delta' theme helped to attract customers. The Charger was joined by a high-performance version of the Coronet – the R/T (road and track). Based on the Coronet 500, the Coronet R/T series used the 375bhp Magnum 440in³ V8 as standard, as

Drag racing champion Al Eckstrand used this 1966 Charger on a European exhibition tour during the mid-1960s. The car is unusual in that it is an ex-press corps example that was given to Eckstrand to take to England for the reopening of Santa Pod Raceway, before the official public release of the Charger mid-season. Fitted with the 426 Hemi-Charger, the car stayed in Europe at the end of the tour until 1999 when Al returned it to the States. Al is pictured here with the car near his home in Naples, Florida.

These two pictures show the radical changes that were going on as the Funny Car evolved. Roger Lindamood's 'Color Me Gone' 1965 Coronet (top) was built by Amblewagon of Detroit, using acid-dipped frames and mainly stock parts. The Hemi-powered, fuel-injected car achieved times in the upper 9 second bracket with speeds in excess of 140mph. Just one year later and 'Color Me Gone' is now a Charger, with many fiberglass panels, but still with a 426in³ Hemi. Runs were down in the 8 second range with speeds topping 160mph. Roger is still active in nostalgia competition today.

Don Garlits, one of drag racing's most colorful and successful racers, known affectionately as 'Big Daddy', roaring off the line in his new for 1966 poppy red 175in wheelbase Dodge-powered 'Wynn's Charger'. Garlits, all-time great Top Fuel champion, was the first dragster pilot to hit 170mph, then 180, and on 12 July 1964 he made history by becoming the first racer to break the vaunted 200mph barrier. The car was powered by a supercharged, fuel-injected 426in³ Hemi-Charger V8.

The Dart models got a drastic restyle for 1967 and looked a lot better for it. The delta theme seen on other Dodge vehicles was used widely this year, and was most noticeable on the Dart's taillight setup. Available as the base Dart, 270 or this top-of-the-range GT, the car could be had with an economical slant-six or a potent V8. The sportiest version was this 383in³-powered GTS. In 1967, 38,225 GTs were sold.

1967 Red Coronet R/T. The Dodge Rebellion was aimed at buyers who wanted maximum performance from the biggest available engines. The 440 Magnum V8 in this Coronet R/T was a very attractive proposition.

well as heavy-duty suspension and brakes.

For 1968 the division underwent another facelift ... except the Charger, which experienced a major transformation. Gone was the fastback with its huge trunk space, for something called a semi-fastback.

The fastback Charger had been introduced in mid-season of 1966 in retaliation to the AMC Marlin, Mustang and Plymouth's Barracuda, and was based very much on the Coronet chassis and body, but style-wise was a complete departure from Dodge's mainstream cars. Hidden headlights and full-width taillights

New for 1967 was the introduction of another all-out performance model, the Coronet R/T. The R/T came fitted with the huge 440 magnum as standard, which offered 375bhp at 4600rpm. A complete power package included heavy-duty suspension with sway bar and uprated shock absorbers, 3in-wide drum brakes with front discs as options, dual exhausts, heavy-duty battery and 14in wheels fitted with 7.75314 Red Streak nylon tires. Special body stripes accentuated the pinched-in waistline with R/T insignia shown on all sides.

For 1967 all Dodges had new styling or a makeover throughout what was one of the fullest ranges in the industry: three compact Dart models, five Coronet, the single model Charger, two full-size Polara lines and two full-size luxury Monaco series. The medium-size Coronet again proved to be Dodge's overwhelming success. It remained on the 117in wheelbase and, because of its re-style the previous year, the '67 changes were mainly in trim detail. A new grille – with thin vertical bars broken up into four large quarters – had the Dodge emblem as a centerpiece. The 500 series shown here is the two-door hardtop coupé fitted with the optional 426 Hemi engine. The base engine for this model was a 383. It was still very much a performance car, but with the emphasis on a new R/T.

1967 Charger. For its second and final year as a fastback, the Charger went virtually unchanged. Extra indicators were mounted on the top of the front fenders; there was a little more body chrome, and a few interior trim changes were made. Base power plant was still the 230bhp 318in³ V8 with options on the 383in², 426 Hemi and the new 440 Magnum. A vinyl roof was now on the options list, too. Sales dropped dramatically to just 15,788; this car is one of only twenty-seven Chargers that were factory-fitted with the highly desirable 426 Hemi.

The Dodge Charger fastback joined the Dodge Rebellion halfway through 1966, but would last just 2 years before a restyle that would see a complete change to the rear and the end of the fastback. This newspaper advert from December 1966 emphasized the powerful options and standard equipment on offer, but failed to entice the public. Only 15,788 buyers went for the Charger in 1967, compared with the very popular restyle for 1968, which sold over 96,000 units.

were just some of the unique Charger touches, and as mentioned, this model carried the awesome Street Hemi. But for 1968 it changed again. The fastback roof line was changed to a more conventional 'flying buttress' style top with a body that matched other Coronets. Fake air scoops were stamped into the door panels (Coronets had theirs stamped into the rear 'Coke bottle' flanks just behind the door) and the hidden headlights remained. At the rear, the deck curved up at the tail to form just a hint of a spoiler set above four round taillights. A competition style chrome 'quick-fill' petrol filler cap sat atop the rear left flank. Designed by William Brownlie, who had penned the Charger concept and '66 production models, this car became an instant classic and it looks as good today as it did back then. Match this body with the Hemi-optioned engine and you have one of the most desirable and most beautiful muscle cars ever built.

Richard Petty in no 43 at Daytona. For the 1967 race season, legendary racing driver Richard Petty used the same Hemi-powered Plymouth Belvedere as he did in 1966. Although aerodynamically challenged, this car, along with team-mate Jim Paschal's Plymouth, stormed through the season. Petty won the drivers' championship with twenty-seven victories and eleven top 5 finishes, and Petty Engineering took thirty-one of the forty-eight Grand National races. This shot shows Petty in no 43 trailing Cale Yarborough's 427in^3 'tunnel port'-powered Ford in the Daytona 500. Mario Andretti went on to win the race in one of Ford's few victories that season in his Holman & Moody-prepped Fairlane.

1967 Daytona Speedway. This is where legends were made. Daytona International Speedway was opened in February 1959. Constructed on 377 acres of ex-Daytona Beach airport land, it was the first ever purpose-built super speedway. The track is shaped into a tri-oval that stretches 2.5 miles, with high banking to allow for faster speeds. The banks are set at 31 degrees, the steepest the builder could attain. The dark oblong in the center of the picture is a lake. This was made by the excavation of earth used in the banking. The small oval to the left in the middle ground is a dog track. Daytona Beach airport can be seen top right of the picture.

If looks alone weren't enough to make it a classic, film immortality certainly did the job. Director Peter Yates used a black Charger in what is arguably the most famous cinematic car chase in history. Steve McQueen's film *Bullitt* saw Lt. Frank Bullitt at the wheel of his 1968 Ford Mustang, being chased through the precipitous streets of San Francisco by the bad guys in a black Charger. Leaping through intersections and screaming around corners, so powerful was the Dodge that it had to be held back. Although the car chase was very inconsistent – the Dodge lost six hubcaps, turned a corner and came out on the other side of town, and of course don't forget the reappearing VW Beetle – this 9 minute 42 second chase became movie history and made the film a box office hit.

Dodge was now advertising the 'Scat Pack'; its selection of performance models. As well as the Coronet R/T and Dart GTS, there was the Charger, now in R/T form. All could be instantly identified by the two Bumblebee stripes, which wrapped around the rear of each Scat Pack car.

For 1967, Dodge and Plymouth brought out a new drag package. The Coronet and Belvedere-based cars were constructed on a very limited basis (fifty of each). A large flat hood scoop was the biggest visual difference outside, while inside there was just a bench seat and roll cage; no radio, heater, body sealer or undercoat was fitted (but things weren't really happening for ChryCo cars at the strip, although Ronnie Sox won the NHRA Spring Nationals). This retro drag racer is based on one of those cars. Shot at Avon Park Raceway in England, 'Wedge-O-Matic' is a 1967 Coronet R/T fitted with a 440in³ mill, matched to a 727 Torqueflite automatic gearbox.

1967 'Wedge-O Matic'. This back shot shows the full-width rear grille that matched the front. Thin plastic vertical bars hid the stop and indicator lights until illuminated. Only available as a two-door hardtop or convertible, this R/T would originally have cost $3199 and weighed in at 3565lb.

1967 'Wedge-O-Matic'. Again, pictured recently at Avon Park Raceway, the huge rear tires of Coronet R/T are warmed up just behind the start line, ready to take on a 1969 Barracuda. The front of the car is secured with a break 'line-lock'. This Coronet regularly runs in the 11 second bracket.

The Dart had a new model line for 1968. The GTS took over from the GT as the top performer. A mild makeover of the 'all-new' 1967 Dart kept the wheelbase at 111in and overall length at 195.4in, and concentrated on a new grille and rear lights. But the GTS also came with fake hood scoops, firm-ride shock absorbers, heavy-duty rally suspension, engine dress-up kit, E70314 Red Streak wide oval tires, and the warning 'bumblebee' stripes across the back of the car. The base engine was the new 340in^3 V8, which gave 275bhp, but at extra cost the 383in^3 V8 was available, giving 300bhp. The GTS was only available as a two-door hardtop or convertible.

The 1968 Coronets received a welcome re-styling that smoothed out some of those flat sides, and accentuated the 'Coke-bottle' waistline. The delta-shape theme featured on all Dodge cars now, and it could be seen on Coronets in the rear lights, fake air scoops and front grille. The 440 was the medium-price offering, selling at $2671 for this new two-door hardtop coupé (fixed B-pillar). On the options list was a vinyl roof in white, black or green.

For advertising purposes, Dodge dubbed its performance cars the 'Scat Pack'. A cartoon bumblebee on wheels helped promote "the cars with the Bumblebee stripes". These are the small Dart GTS (top), medium-sized Coronet R/T (middle) and Charger R/T (bottom). As can be seen in this press shot, the stripes encircled the whole of the rear end, warning potential rivals on the street not to tangle with Dodge's '68 'go-mobiles'!

FORD GETS AERODYNAMIC

The 1968 NASCAR race season kicked off with engines going pretty much unchanged, and Mopar drivers feeling pretty smug and confident of another successful year. What they hadn't counted on was Ford's new aerodynamic cars. Ford's Tunnel-Port 427 Wedge could kick out 600bhp – but in the right hands so could Chrysler's Hemi, so it was pretty evenly matched. However, when the new Ford Fairlanes and Torinos, and Mercury Montegos and Cyclones hit the track, they had up to 10mph advantages on the ChryCo cars. Even Petty's super-tuned Plymouth was 5mph slower than the slowest FoMoCo car. The Mercury Cyclone could better 193mph around the track against Dodge and Plymouth's 183 and 184mph.

This picture of a 1968 Coronet 440 clearly shows the delta-shaped rear lights held within a full-length concave escutcheon. The standard engine was a 225in³ slant-six or a mild 273.5in³ V8. This car has non-standard wheels and tires, and has had the 'bumblebee' stripes added. These were not generally available on non-Scat Pack vehicles.

CORONET 440

This head-on shot of a 1968 Coronet R/T is the image you might briefly see in your rear view mirror just before it blew past you. Menacingly low and wide, it is revealing exterior gauges which are another clue that this is not a car to mess with. The original white turn signals mounted in the bumper have been colored amber to meet British legislation.

1968 Coronet R/T. This original press shot from Dodge public relations shows the start of that beautiful 'Coke-bottle' styling with the pinched-in waistline. The R/T, along with all other Coronets, had the two fake air scoops stamped into its rear panels. The '68s remained on the 117in chassis that they shared with the Charger. The Coronet was the most successful line for Dodge that year with total sales of 213,635 units. Of these, 10,849 were R/Ts.

Bullitt. The film made cinematic history with its incredible car chase and helped make the Mustang GT390 a popular car. The black 440in³-powered '68 Charger fared much worse in the chase, being forced off the road and exploding. Driven by famed stunt driver Bill Hickman, the Charger easily out-powered and out-maneuvered the Mustang, but Steve McQueen in the Mustang had to come out on top, promoting the Ford to 'classic' status and relegating the superior Charger into the 'has been' class.

Dodge and Plymouth engineers hadn't been idle, though. Both divisions' products had smoother bodies, and the Charger especially looked perfect for the oval track with its new semi-fastback styling. However, it had two major flaws: the recessed grill had turned into an air brake, and the recessed, almost vertical rear windshield caused air turbulence, making the cars incredibly hard to steer at NASCAR race speeds.

Buddy Baker managed to chalk up a win when he took his Ray Fox prepped Charger to victory in the World 600 race, as did Charlie Glotzbach at the National 500 (Charlotte) in his Cotton Owens Charger. Throughout the whole season Dodge went down victory lane only five times. Ford took twenty wins of the total forty-nine races. Mercury had seven, Plymouth did well to get sixteen and Chevy, which had started to take an interest in racing again in '67, managed one win. Mother Mopar wasn't happy. This was the start of the 'aero war'.

But at the drag strip, Mopar still dominated. For the '68 season only, the 426in³ Hemi was shoehorned into the small A-bodied Dart. With the

STEVE McQUEEN

"BULLITT"

UNE PRODUCTION SOLAR

ROBERT VAUGHN

JACQUELINE BISSET

DON GORDON
ROBERT DUVALL
SIMON OAKLAND
NORMAN FELL
TECHNICOLOR

The Chargers were all new for 1968. Completely redesigned, the fastback had been replaced by a fresh semi-fastback or 'flying buttress' back end and a more Coronet-looking body. Hidden headlamps sat behind a recessed grille that would cause problems on the race track, but sales were impressive. Just over 96,000 cars were sold.

crossram Hemi intake, Holley carbs and a compression ratio of 12.5:1, the results were startling. Making the most of the ultra-lightweight body and fiberglass panels, Ronnie Sox won both NHRA and AHRA World Titles, while independent drivers and factory-backed teams were also taking wins around America.

The 1969 GT was the luxury offering in the small Dart range. It was available in only two body styles – the convertible and this handsome two-door hardtop. Special to these cars was the high body side-trim, blacked-out front grille and GT badging. The base engine was still a 115bhp six, but a 273.5in³ or 318in³ V8 could be selected at extra cost.

6 THE AERO WAR 1969-1971

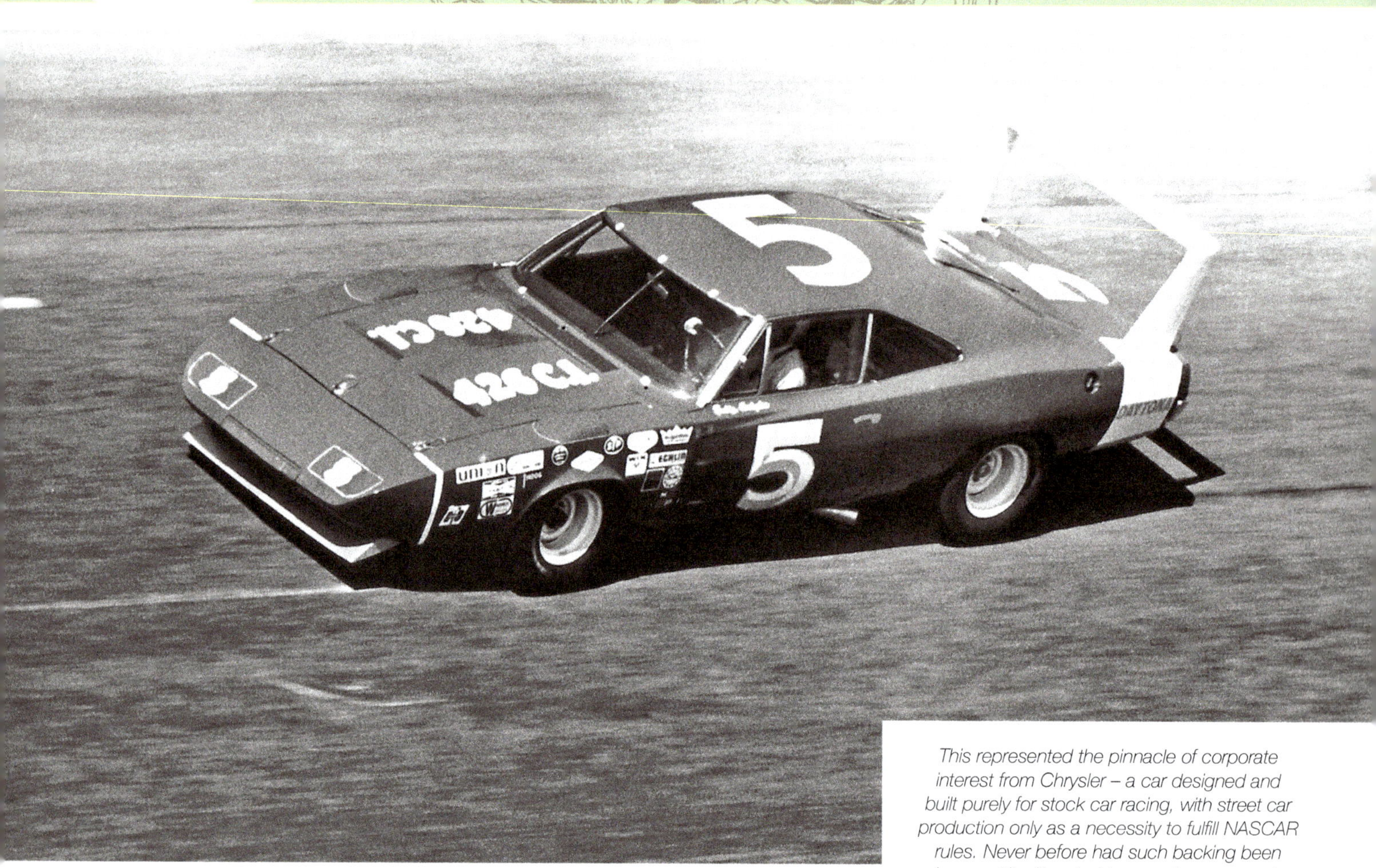

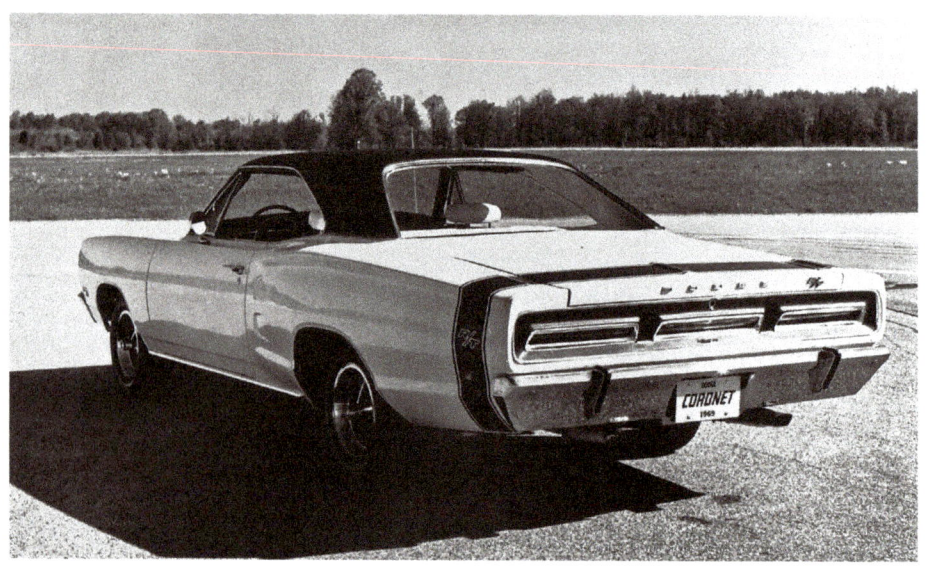

This represented the pinnacle of corporate interest from Chrysler – a car designed and built purely for stock car racing, with street car production only as a necessity to fulfill NASCAR rules. Never before had such backing been given and it will probably never be seen again, but the result was the most radical yet elegant race car ever to circle the Super Speedways of America. This is Buddy Arrington, one of many owner-drivers, in his no 5 Dodge Charger Daytona.

The Coronet R/T was still looked upon as the main performance car from Dodge. The '69 models underwent a mild facelift that saw less emphasis on the delta theme. Three long rear taillights now filled the escutcheon under the trunk lip, and there was a very slight revision of the front grille. A wider bumblebee stripe held the R/T logo. Only two choices of engine were on offer to R/T buyers: the powerful 440in^3 Magnum came as base engine, with the 426 Hemi as an extra option.

1969 Coronet SuperBee. The SuperBee was introduced mid-season 1968 as an affordable alternative to the R/T. A no-frills performance package within the base Coronet series, it came as either a two-door coupé or two-door hardtop. A modified 383in³ V8 supplied the power, although the 390bhp 440 Six-Pack motor was optional and only available on the SuperBee. Four-speed manual or Torqueflite auto transmissions were options, with power supplied to the rear wheels via a Dana 60 back axle. This two-door hardtop has the 383 fitted.

The full-size Dodge Polara and Monaco models received a new 'fuselage' body which, although still looking very slab-sided, had rounded off some of the right angles of previous years and gave a more massive appearance. The smaller Coronet and Dart models continued to be the performance cars. The Coronets got a makeover to the front grille, taillights and interior, but 1969 model also saw the introduction of the SuperBee, released mid-way through 1968. This was a basic no-frills Coronet that made owning a Mopar muscle car affordable. The price tag of just $3027 allowed for

Exclusive to the 1969 SuperBee was the option of this 440 Six-Pack. The engine featured three in-line, two-barrel Holley carburetors on top of an Edelbrock aluminum manifold. The aim was to achieve reasonable fuel economy with exceptional performance when required. While the vehicles were being lightly driven, only one of the three carbs would operate, but under heavy acceleration all carbs would kick in. From a standing start these engines could out-accelerate a Hemi-powered Coronet up to 70mph, then the Hemi's superior breathing would win through.

very few creature comforts, but did include a nice 383 Magnum that used 440 heads and a stronger cam, and a bumblebee stripe as standard on either a 2-door hardtop or 2-door coupé. They were incredibly popular and over 27,800 were sold. The famous 'Six-Pak' was brought in late in the '69 model year, for use on 1969½ and 1970 cars. Offered on the 340 and 440in^3 engines, in essence it was an Edelbrock aluminum manifold with three Holley 2-barrel carbs bolted on top. The idea was to obtain economy along with performance. When driven lightly, only one of the three carbs would operate for maximum fuel efficiency, but when extra power was required all three would kick in, giving more horsepower overall. It was a very successful setup and is still very popular with Mopar fans today.

The compact Dart models remained one of the best sellers and like the Coronets, were treated to a facelift of new front grille, rear lights and trim detail. Also like the Coronet, the Dart received a new series – the Dart Swinger 340. This was much like the SuperBee insomuch as it was intended as an affordable performance car. Predictably, it came with the 275bhp 340in^3 V8 and had a 4-speed manual gearbox, heavy-duty

The SuperBee's 440 Six-Pack engine featured many high-performance parts including higher load valve springs, low taper camshaft and flat face tappets, dual breaker distributor, molybdenum-filled top piston rings and viscous drive fan. The most obvious clue to the presence of a Six-Pack was the matt-black glass fiber competition hood, complete with air scoop, that was held in place with four hood pins.

This imposing front view of the 1969 Coronet SuperBee shows how low and wide the cars were. The smart, functional hood scoops were an optional extra. The power bulge hood from the Coronet R/T was the usual fitment.

The Dart Swinger 340 was a new model for 1969. Sold as an economical version of the GTS, the Swinger came in only one body style – a two-door hardtop. A true compact performance offering from Dodge, its standard equipment included the 340in³ V8 with a four-speed manual shift gearbox, heavy-duty suspension, the GTS hood, bumblebee stripe, and D70 tires. The Dart series remained one of Dodge's best-sellers.

'Family-styled sports car' – that's what Dodge advertising said about the slightly restyled Charger for 1969. They must have been very fast-moving families. This Charger is fitted with the 426in³ Street Hemi, although a 225in³ slant-six was the base engine. Retractable headlamps remained, but now sat within a split front grille.

suspension, power bulge hood and D70x14 wide oval tires as standard. The 383 Magnum was available at extra cost.

The Charger kicked off the year with the same two lines – the base Charger, then Charger R/T. These cars carried only minor facelifts. Mid-season saw the Charger 500 released. This was based on the race version of the Charger, and for homologation purposes Dodge promised to make at least 500 of these cars. Although no exact numbers have ever been released, unconfirmed factory figures speak of 505 cars being built, but it is thought that in reality the total didn't exceed 392. However, this was the first time that a US manufacturer had ever created a car line just so it could compete in a specific type of motorsport. So what was different about the 500 and how did it do at the track?

Dodge made over 89,000 Chargers in 1969, and only about 500 of these were fitted with the base 225in³ slant-six. The more popular choice by far was the 230bhp 318in³ V8. The 383in³ V8 was also on the extras list of base Chargers. All R/T models came with a 440in³ V8 with a four-barrel carb as standard that, like this one, gave out 375bhp. The 426in³ Hemi was optional on the R/T.

The inspiration for The Dukes of Hazzard *was a 1975 film called* The Moonrunners, *in which a close-knit, backwoods family set out to produce and sell its own moonshine despite interruptions from the law and competitors. For the TV show, it was agreed that a fast car was needed, and the '69 Charger was chosen because of its racing success.*

One of the most famous cars on American TV screens must be the General Lee, from the Warner Bros series The Dukes of Hazzard. *The car is a 1969 Dodge Charger. With its distinctive rebel flag on the roof and 01 racing number on the doors, it is hard to mistake it for any other.*

FORD TAKES FIRST BLOOD

After tasting defeat in the '68 stock car series, Dodge executives drafted in a team of Chrysler engineers to fix the problem. Working from a sketch by engineer John Pointer, the team, headed by Gary Romberg (borrowed from Chrysler's Space Division) and Bob Marcell, went about putting the theory into practice. A flush mounted grille insert was sealed in position for the front-end problem, and a sheet of metal was used to fill the hole between the top of the C-pillar and the bottom of the buttress to make a fastback roof line. A smaller rear windshield was sealed to this. Wind tunnel tests gave favorable results, so production of the Charger 500 was authorised.

The production 500s came with a 440 as standard, but of course the racers had the 426 Hemi. So, as the 1969 season came about Dodge drivers, at least, seemed eager to go. Not so the Plymouth drivers, however. They had to make do with last year's slab-sided styling. NASCAR king, Richard Petty, was particularly upset and requested a transfer from Plymouth to Dodge for the '69 season. Not wanting to lose its star driver, Plymouth refused, so Petty joined Ford instead. This was a major blow to Plymouth and tragic for Mopar fans. But as things would turn out, it was a blessing in disguise. The season kicked off with a

surprise for everybody. The Holman & Moody camp had been secretly working on an aerodynamic car, too – a version of Ford's Fairlane. It was called the Torino Talladega, named after the new super speedway track being built in Alabama, and boy, was it fast! It won the Daytona 500, and almost everything in sight until stable mate Mercury brought out its aero car, the Cyclone Spoiler II, which proved to be even faster than the Talladegas. If this wasn't bad enough, Ford was finally allowed to race its Boss 429in^3 motors. Dodge did pick up some wins on short-track events and had one super speedway win at Daytona in a 100-mile qualifier, but

The General may have appeared indestructible to the viewer, but this was because there were usually three or four versions on set at any one time. As soon as a car had carried out a death-defying jump, it was retired. It is estimated that over 200 1969 Chargers were used in the making of the shows.

the season definitely belonged to Ford.

With a supreme sense of urgency, the Dodge engineers went back to the drawing board. Desperate times called for desperate measures. Their goal was to come up with a winning car for the inaugural Alabama super speedway race in September of 1969. They had just seven months to come up with a design, ensure it worked and then make at least five hundred production cars to fill NASCAR rulings. What they came up with was nothing short of the most radical race car ever seen on a NASCAR track – the Dodge Daytona.

John Pointer again came up with a working sketch of what to do. He and Bob Marcell from the Special Vehicles Department worked on the fine details then submitted the idea to Bob McCurry, Dodge Vice-President, for the okay. They got it. Clay scale models were used in wind tunnel tests, then a full-size clay nose cone was attached to a 1968 Charger. Secret wind tunnel tests of this car

The restyled '69 Chargers had a new rear taillight setup. Gone were the four round pods, replaced by these two longer lights, which held the stop, side and turn signals. The back-up lights can be seen below the bumper. The UK registration number on this R/T is a great way to inform potential rivals which power house lurks under the hood.

After humiliation at the hands of Ford in the 1968 NASCAR season, Dodge engineers were set the task of finding and fixing the problems with the Charger. The solution was the Charger 500 race car. A Coronet front grille with exposed headlights was mounted flush with the front end, and a sheet of metal holding a smaller rear windshield plugged the gap between the top of the C-pillar and the bottom of the buttress, forming a fastback roofline. These measures worked, but Ford's advancements in aerodynamics made the vehicles obsolete almost immediately.

cars had to have a fully opening trunk, so the final height of 23in gave just enough clearance.

Track testing began and the results were incredible. With the new steel nose cone and wing in place, the cars were recorded as getting 200lb of positive downforce at the front of the car and over 600lb at the rear. Handling, of course, was greatly improved, but this brought out another problem. At race speeds, such downforce caused the front tires to rub on the top of the fenders. There was no time to make new fenders so John Pointer simply cut holes in the top of each one and covered it with a rear facing air scoop. Rumours abounded of the scoops helping the aerodynamics and brake cooling but Pointer still maintains today that they were purely for tire clearance. After some fine adjustments to the new setup, Charlie Glotzbach had taken the car up to a staggering 243mph around the banked sections of Chrysler's Chelsea Proving Grounds.

So the team had successfully accomplished its goal. The car was ready for the Alabama 500 and this

were carried out at the Lockheed aircraft site in Georgia. The famous tail fin was going through the same process. Aerodynamics expert Gary Romberg was again brought in, and it was he who came up with the general configuration used on the production car. After much testing, his idea of using the uprights as airfoils and the crossmember as an inverted airfoil were set. But how high to have the uprights? Many heights were suggested and tried, but the deciding factor was very simple. The street

This was the cause of all the fuss over aerodynamics: Ford's new Torino Talladega. When the 1969 NASCAR season kicked off, Dave Pearson took this car to the highest qualifying speed for the Daytona 500 race, with a lap time of 190.029mph. He also won his qualifying 100 mile race. The aerodynamic Talladegas, along with Mercury's Cyclone Spoiler IIs, were the scourge of the Super Speedways. Pearson won the 1969 drivers' title with this car.

To gain aerodynamic supremacy on the race track, the engineers at Dodge came up with the outlandish Charger Daytona. Built by Creative Industries on behalf of Dodge, the steel nose cone and radical rear tail were fitted to the Charger 500 and created what must be the most distinctive silhouette of any production car in the world. To meet NASCAR homologation rules, at least 500 of these vehicles had to be produced for the cars to be allowed to race. The production total reached 505.

Although the new winged Charger Daytonas debuted on the race track in early 1969, it wasn't until the last race of the season in December that Dodge finally managed to beat the Fords and Mercurys. Bobby Isaac won the Texas 500 in his no 71 K&K Insurance Dodge.

was what everybody had so eagerly waited for – the first confrontation between the aero warriors. But it turned out to be a major anti-climax. Talladega's freshly laid cement track was found to be sub-standard, and as the teams began to run qualifying laps the uneven surface began to cause tire ruptures and extreme discomfort to the drivers. The PDA (Professional Drivers Association), not happy with NASCAR chairman Bill France's attitude, went on strike. The race was run with a mish-mash of cars from various classes. The only Daytona drivers not to stay away were Bobby Isaac and Richard Brickhouse. Isaac set a new NASCAR record in his qualifying laps with a run of 199.386mph in his red #71 K&K

Insurance Dodge, and led the strange field for a lot of the race, but it was Brickhouse, making only his second Grand National start, that won the race in Charlie Glotzbach's new #99 Daytona. No Ford aero cars raced that day so the win was a hollow victory for Dodge.

The first real contest between the rival manufacturers wasn't until the National 500 held at Charlotte Motor Speedway. Dodge's expected whitewash never happened. Ford took the first four pole positions and led for most of the race and it was Donnie Allison in a long nosed Talladega that took the checkered flag. So first blood in the aero wars went to FoMoCo. The Dodge drivers unanimously blamed poor tires for

their defeat. However, things didn't improve for Dodge drivers at the next meeting in Rockingham. Ford came in 1st and 2nd, with Buddy Baker in his #6 Daytona coming in 3rd but a whole six laps behind the Fords. It wasn't until the last race of the season in December '69 that Dodge first beat the new Fords. The race was the Texas 500. Buddy Baker led for most of the race until he rammed into another Dodge Daytona driven by James Hylton. The crash cost Baker the race, but Bobby Isaac took up the baton to bring his Daytona home in first place, two laps ahead of the next car, a Talladega. Dodge got the race, but Ford won the 1969 season very decisively. Things would change again for the 1970 season.

AERO WARRIORS FIGHT BACK

Dodge entered the new decade in a buoyant mood. Although sales had dropped, this was an industry-wide trend, so Dodge kept its position in the manufacturers' pecking order. Most of Dodge's models received a makeover, but some new lines and a new performance car gave hope of a good year to come.

The compact Dart was still one of the most popular choices with the economically and performance-minded buyer. Although it used the same body and wheelbase as the '69 Darts, a new rakish front end and sloping rear end gave the cars extra length but also a whole new look. The base Dart, with its economical 125bhp, 198in³ slant six was the one to buy if you were quite frugal, but for power, the GT and GTS had been dropped, leaving the Swinger 340 as the only Dart performance option which now became the compact member of the Scat Pack. With the demise of the GT and GTS lines, this also meant the end of a compact convertible although soft top Polaras and Coronets would still be available until the end of the year.

The mid-size Coronets got a facelift that smoothed out their bodies even more, and saw an unusual front end that had two large delta/oval-shaped openings with heavy chrome surrounds reminiscent of the Pontiac front grille. The base Coronet Deluxe series also included the SuperBee again as a cheaper option for the power hungry, and came with a 383 Magnum as a standard fitment. Intermediate trim level was the 440 series and at the top came the 500 series, including the performance R/T model.

The Coronet-based Charger went virtually unchanged but was now available in three lines – the base Charger, the Charger 500, and finally the new Charger R/T. The R/T came with a 440 magnum and was a

The Dart range looked all-new for 1970. With a fresh, more rakish front end and redesigned rear, it was hard to tell that this was the same body used in previous years. The Dart Swinger 340 was the top performance choice, earning its bumblebee stripes to become part of the Dodge Scat Pack.

The Swinger 340 was only available as a two-door hardtop, and came with the 340in³ V8 engine and a performance setup that included dual exhausts with chrome tips, front disc brakes, heavy-duty suspension, Firm Ride shock absorbers, a 3:23 rear axle ratio, three-speed manual transmission, two hood scoops, and the obligatory Scat Pack bumblebee stripe. This Swinger has a full competition roll cage and fiberglass hood with a single large scoop.

demon performer. A special luxurious trim package was optional on the 500s and R/Ts, called the SE (Special Edition). Hood-mounted indicators, deep-dish wheel covers, leather bucket seats and wood-grained steering wheel made up some of the items found on the SE's build sheet.

Biggest news from Dodge was the introduction of its new pony car, the Challenger. Made to go head-to-head with Ford's great-

This close-up shows the two large oval-shaped openings that made up the front bumper and grille of the 1970 Coronet R/T. Black plastic vertical strips filled the space to the inside of the headlamps. Turn signals were positioned underneath the main grille as well as on the front fenders. Competition type hood tie-pins were optional.

The Coronet received a facelift in 1970 that concentrated mainly on the front grille. This consisted of a very Pontiac-looking twin oval affair with each oval housing a pair of headlamps.

The all-new Challenger shared its fresh E-body platform with Plymouth's new 'Cuda, but Dodge utilized a wheelbase that was 2in longer than its 108in Plymouth cousin. Available in two series, the base Challenger and R/T, it had only three body styles: two-door hardtop, two-door coupé or convertible. The rear end featured one long, deep escutcheon that met the rear bumper. Twin exhausts finished at squared-off quad tips.

The Challenger's interior was well laid out. Vinyl bucket seats sat each side of a center console that held the gearshift stick. This R/T has the SE option package which came with a full Rallye instrument cluster, as well as a performance hood, heavy-duty suspension and vinyl roof.

selling Mustang, Mercury's Cougar and GM's Camaro, the Challenger was closely related to Plymouth's slippery 'Cuda' and had the now well established 'coke-bottle' body that was accentuated by the raised rear fenders. They sat on a 110in wheelbase and came as either 2-door hardtops or convertibles. A plush SE model was available but the real performer was the R/T model. All the usual heavy-duty parts were there along with a 383in^3 V8 fitted with a 4-barrel carb. Optional was the 425hp Street Hemi, which was now using hydraulic instead of solid valve lifters, and came with a 'shaker' hood and a price tag of $779. Because Chrysler wished to enter the new Trans-America race series, Dodge offered a Challenger T/A. Similar to Plymouth's AAR (All American Racers) 'Cuda, the T/A had a 340 Six-Pak engine and came with a functional hood scoop, NASCAR-style hood pins, unique T/A side stripes, competition quick-fill petrol cap and rear spoiler. Challengers were a limited success in an already diminishing market, with 63,094 base models and 19,938 R/Ts

(including T/As) being built. The rarest Challenger must be the convertible R/T factory fitted with a 426 Hemi. Only nine of these were ever built.

In competition, Dodge had a fantastic year. While the new Challenger T/A driven by Sam Posey in the SCCA Trans-Am series could

ChryCo became interested in the Trans-Am racing series for a brief period, and released a mid-year model to coincide with this. This is the 1970 Challenger T/A (Trans-Am) prototype, which went unchanged for the production model. The air scoop is secured with competition hood pins.

only make 4th place, the 'winged warriors' had a more successful season altogether. I mentioned earlier that race-king Richard Petty's defection to Ford in 1969 was, in some ways, a blessing, and the reason is that without the liaison with Ford, there would never have been a Plymouth Superbird. Plymouth was so eager to get Petty back, it gave in to his demands for a winged warrior of his own. The hastily-built Superbirds looked very similar to the Dodge Daytona, but were built around the Plymouth Road Runner. Not having time to re-invent an all-new aero car, Plymouth modified Dodges front fenders to fit its car, changing the shape of the nose cone slightly at the same time. A taller, more swept-back tail wing was fitted and some body plugging was needed around the rear windshield. NASCAR rules had changed. They had increased production limits to at least 1000 units. As it turned out,

The 1970 Challenger T/A came with a 340in^3 V8 as standard along with the functional hood scoop, rear spoiler, competition quick-fill fuel cap, blacked-out hood and special side stripes. Racer Sam Posey campaigned a Challenger T/A in the SCCA Trans-Am series but could only manage fourth position.

The 1970 T/A mid-season special had a toughened 340 Six-Pack V8, sport suspension and a four-speed manual gearbox. The unique side stripes were standard, as were the engine identification stickers on the front fenders.

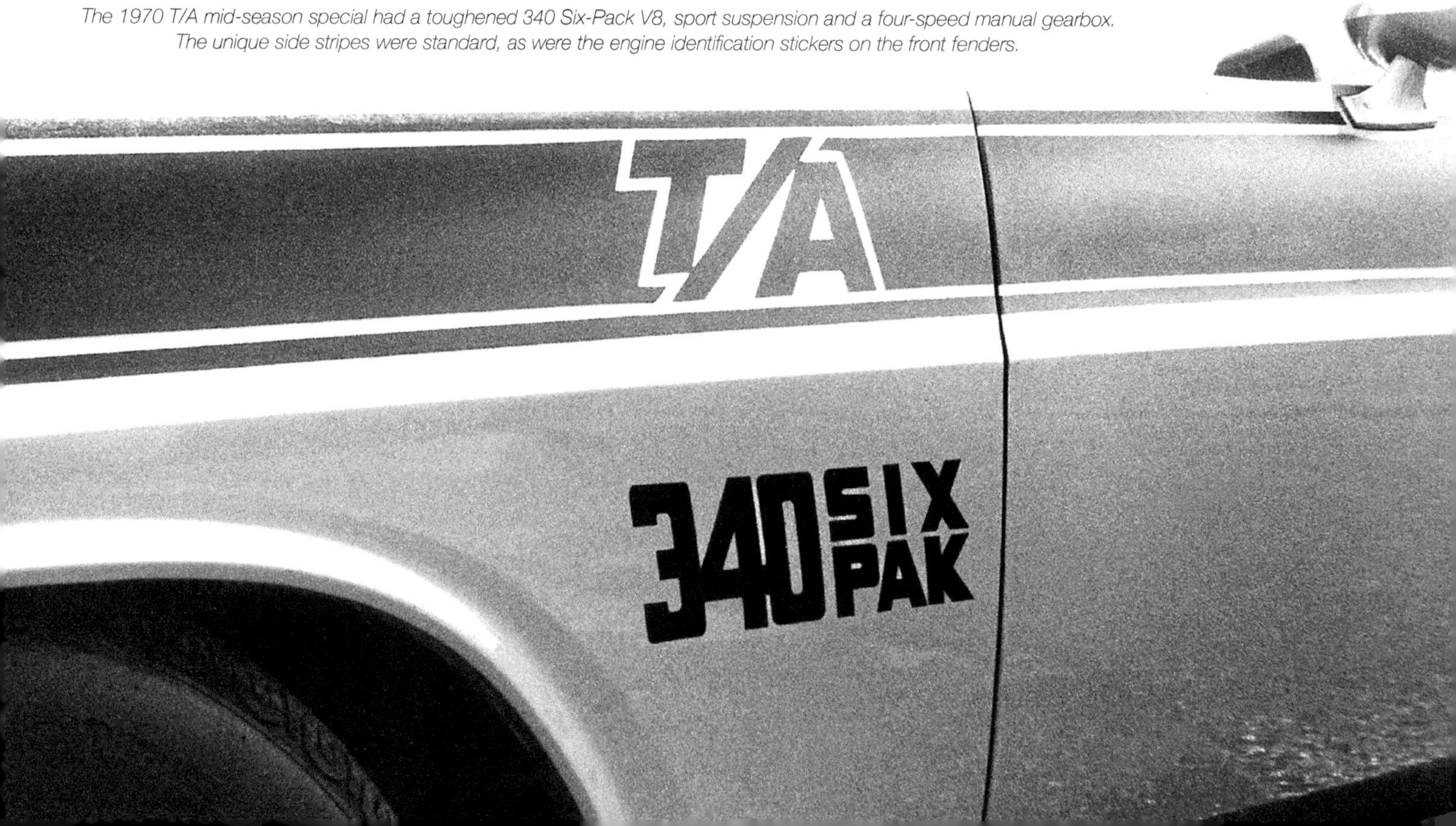

The 1970 Chargers had changed very little from those of the previous year, but did see an addition to the line-up with the introduction of the Charger 500. Not to be confused with the race Charger 500 from '69, this 500 was a well optioned base vehicle that came with a 230bhp 318in³ V8. A 'Special Edition' (SE) package could be had on 500 and R/T models.

The badge on the side of the functional hood scoops says it all ...

This period advert shows one of the 1070 Challenger R/T convertibles made for 1970. Side stripes or bumblebee stripes on the tail were optional. Another 3173 base Challengers were built that year.

The 1970 Chargers had changed very little from those of the previous year, but there was an addition to the line-up with the introduction of the Charger 500. Not to be confused with the race Charger 500 from '69, this 500 was a well-optioned base Charger that came with a 230bhp 318in³ V8. A 'Special Edition' (SE) package could be had on the 500 and R/T models.

production of these cars surpassed that by a large margin.

So, when the 1970 season kicked off at Riverside Raceway in California there were two types of Mopar winged cars to battle with the FoMoCo aero cars. Ford drivers were in a bad situation. Lee Iacocca, a name known to many Mopar fans as the saviour of the Chrysler Corporation in the late seventies, and the man usually associated with the success of the Mustang in 1964, had just been promoted to chief executive at Ford. One of the first decisions he made was to cut race funding by a massive 75 per cent. The planned Torino King Cobra and Mercury Super Spoiler never got past the prototype stage and left Ford drivers using last year's cars. However, the Mopar driver's confidence took a large knock when A J Foyt won that first race in his Ford Torino, and in the first of two qualifying 100-mile races at Daytona, Cale Yarborough took his Mercury Spoiler to the winners circle. The Ford underdog seemed to be biting back. Although seriously under-funded, running low on parts and using last season's cars, Ford was still winning.

Charlie Glotzbach won the second Daytona 500 qualifier to even the score a little, and Pete Hamilton took his Petty Engineering-prepped Superbird across the line in the main race (Petty blew his engine on the 7th lap), making this the first win for a Plymouth winged car. The whole season was closely fought. Petty won the next Super speedway meet in his Superbird and Bobby Allison notched up a win for Dodge at Atlanta in his Daytona. FoMoCo drivers clawed back wins in the Rebel

1970 Chargers had a deeper chrome surround/ front bumper than the '69 models, but still had hidden headlamps, now behind plastic covers that featured two long, horizontal ovals holding thin vertical veins. Side turn signals remained below the main grille.

This rare 1970 Charger R/T is owned and has been restored by Chrysler. Although over 10,000 R/Ts were built in 1970, only 232, including this one, were fitted with a 426in³ Hemi engine. They came with a 375bhp 440 Magnum V8 as standard (a 390bhp version was available). Many buyers couldn't see the point of paying the extra $648 for the 426 Hemi when the 440 Magnum was such a powerful performer.

400 at Darlington, the World 600, the Motor State 400 in Michigan and the Firecracker 400, then an astounding run of wins saw Daytona's and Superbirds take the next 19 straight victories.

Ford Motor Company drivers picked up wins at the National 500 and the American 500 but as the dust settled on the 1970 NASCAR season, it was Dodge driver Bobby Isaac who took the championship, with 11 wins and 47 starts from the 48 races. ChryCo won the maker's title with 17 Dodge wins and 21 for Plymouth. Ford and Mercury could only manage ten between them. The end of the season also marked the end of an era. Ford quit motorsport completely. Holman & Moody continued to support Ford drivers and cars and Ford still made some competition parts, but Ford didn't offer any direct support to teams. With the competition dispatched, Chrysler also scaled down its motorsport operation and kept Petty engineering as its main focal point. NASCAR once again changed the competition rules, reducing engine sizes and outlawing modified cars – in effect banning Ford's aero

Although the Charger Daytona was a product of 1969, its finest moments came in the 1970 season. This great shot shows a gaggle of winged warriors led by Richard Brickhouse (no 14) and Richard Petty (no 43) early in the Daytona 500 in Florida. Petty's team-mate Pete Hamilton went on to win the race in a Superbird no 40.

For the 1970 season eighteen separate teams fielded Dodge Daytonas. Here, Bobby Allison in no 22 trails Buddy Baker's no 6 Daytona in the Atlanta 500. Allison won this race and also scored wins at short track events at Bristol, Tennessee, and Hampton, Virginia.

One of the most famous and successful cars was this K&K Insurance team Daytona, driven by Bobby Isaac (no 71). Bobby took the drivers' championship in 1970 with eleven wins and forty-seven starts from the forty-eight races. But this marked the end of an era. Ford withdrew from motorsport at the end of 1970, so Chrysler downscaled its interests, too. NASCAR engine and car size rulings for 1971 made it impossible for Daytonas to race competitively. It was a short but exciting life for the winged warriors.

In its heyday Grand-Spaulding Dodge in Chicago was the largest performance Dodge dealership on the planet. One way that the owner, 'Mr Norm' Krause (bottom) kept the business in the limelight was with a string of Funny Cars. For 1970, the Gary Dyer driven vehicle (top) had a Challenger-bodied entry. By this time, Funny Cars had developed into a major part of the fabric of drag racing and were no longer considered side-show attractions. By the mid-1970s, Dyer was achieving high 6 second times in this car. (Photograph originally Dodge Spalding, courtesy Geoff Stunkard)

cars and ChryCo's 'winged warriors' from competing.

So the Superbirds and Daytonas had beaten the Talladegas and Cyclones, but perhaps it was not as great a victory as it could have been. Was it so hard to beat last year's

cars, especially when those teams had little backing from Ford? Yes, the competition could have been stiffer perhaps, but it was still the Dodge Daytona's finest hour.

At the drag strip, top fuel champion Don 'Big Daddy' Garlits

was seriously injured when his front engine configured drag car exploded. Miraculously, he survived and went on to create the safer rear engine top fuel dragster, eventually revolutionising the sport.

MUSCLE CARS FADE AWAY

It wasn't just the end of an era for motorsport, though – it was the beginning of the end of the muscle car war. The first shots had been fired by insurance companies, who were now starting to hike up premiums to astronomical levels for powerful cars. Politics was also playing a bigger role, with noises about pollution and the environment getting louder. The trend was for smaller cars with lower-powered engines that could run on either regular or unleaded petrol as emission-control standards were tightened. Chrysler's performance division didn't make its engines any larger, but it didn't make them any smaller either. Dodge had the advantage of having a great array of engines available, from the 198in^3 slant six up to the massive 440 Magnum V8, but was well aware of the changing market so introduced its first captive import in 1971: the Mitsubishi-built Colt – the divisions answer to a sub-compact.

Dodge's new Demon brings out the devil in you.

Based very much on the Plymouth Duster, the 1971 Demon 340 was Dodge's latest compact performance car. It was part of the Dart series but was smaller than standard Darts. As the name suggests, the car came equipped with a 340in^3 V8 that was good for 275bhp, matched to a three-speed manual transmission. Rallye suspension, E70314 tires and a floor-mounted gear shifter also came as part of the 340 package.

The Charger received a complete redesign for 1971. Available in three series – the base Charger, Charger 500 (pictured) and top-of-the-range R/T – they all sat on a new 115in chassis and were of a semi-fastback design. The deep front bumper/grille surround now split in two and the Charger's telltale hidden headlamps were replaced with fixed quad headlamps. The standard engine was either a 225in^3 slant-six or a 318in^3 V8 mated to a three-speed manual transmission.

CHARGER Super Bee
Even with a 383 Magnum...it's a regular gas.

1971 Charger SuperBee advert. All Chargers sat on a new 115in wheelbase chassis and the range expanded to five hardtops and one coupé across three series. The Charger SuperBee was part of the '500' series and followed in the footsteps of the Coronet SuperBee of the previous year, offering a low-priced, high-performance setup. The SuperBee was only available as a 2-door hardtop and came with heavy-duty brakes and shocks, F70x14 belted black sidewall tires with raised white letters, Rallye suspension and instrument cluster, a floor-mounted 3-speed manual transmission and 275bhp version of the 383in^3 V8 as standard. This was the only year that a SuperBee appeared on a Charger, and of the 32,114 Chargers built for 1971, only 5054 carried the SuperBee package.

CHARGER R/T
This car was designed strictly for adults.

With ever-increasing premiums for insurance, the days of the muscle car were numbered. The Charger R/T was in its final year but still offered a great-looking package with power to match. The base 440 Magnum could be optioned up for a 440 Six Pack or the 426 Hemi. Vented hood, blacked-out grille and mock air vents on the doors distinguished the R/T from the other models. A Ramcharger hood was optional for 1971.

The Challenger underwent a minor facelift for 1971 which concentrated on a revised front grille and rear lights, along with a few trim changes. Challenger sales dipped dramatically this season, however – down from the previous year's 83,032 total to just 29,883. Larger and more expensive than its Ford rivals, the Challenger was entering an already diminishing market.

The Dart was still perceived to be the main contender in the small-car market, and not wanting to damage a successful formula went virtually unchanged from 1970. However, an all-new Dart model was introduced – the Dart Demon. Due to its Plymouth Duster basis, the Demon coupé was shorter than the normal Darts and had a smaller, 108in wheelbase. With its high rear end, it did have a much more modern look and shared a similarity with some other Dodge series. The Scat-Pack was still prowling, and the new line had the Demon 340 model. The more boxy Darts still had the attractive Swinger and stripped down Swinger Specials for 'scatting' around in.

Dodge's medium-sized Coronets were smoothed out and an unusual full-width, integrated front grill/bumper was introduced to give a 'gapping mouth' effect which looked a lot like last year's Charger grille. The Coronet models took a large step back from the performance image that they once held, and handed it squarely over to the Charger and Challenger lines. The Coronets stretched out in size and were now only available as 4-door sedans and station wagons. The similarities between the Charger and Coronets dwindled too, as for the first time Chargers used a different wheelbase from Coronets. The Charger wheelbase shrunk to 115in as the Coronet's grew to 118in.

Along with a shorter wheelbase, Chargers also got a complete re-style to further separate them from the Coronet line. There were six models within three series – the base Charger, the Charger 500, and R/T. The SuperBee was part of the 500 series. All Chargers were semi-fastback coupes, and featured a full-width front grille/bumper that was now split vertically in two. The rear of the car had a slight spoiler and six distinctive square taillights set in to the long oval rear bumper. The SuperBee and R/T models remained in the 'Pack' as performance models. Base engine for a Charger was the 318in^3 V8 at 230bhp. Standard on the SuperBee was the 383in^3 V8, which gave 275 horses, and the R/T came with the 440 Magnum with 370bhp. Optional across the three series were

The base Challenger line offered the only convertible in the Dodge range. The 1971 model was almost unchanged from the previous year. Only 2165 were made. This would be the last year that Dodge offered a soft-top.

CHALLENGER R/T
It ain't Attila the Hun, but it ain't Mary Mild either.

This sharp-looking piece of iron is designed to run on regular gas. Do not think, however, that this indicates that you'll have to beat it with a whip to get it out of the garage.

Challenger R/T is more than a respectable performer. The 383 Magnum touches a very impressive horse-power figure and stays there with a minimum of tuning. The suspension is done right, the shift is full-synchro and floor-mounted, the interior is still a little roomier and better-looking than some others you've seen, and the Standard Equipment List is darn near as long as the options.

A guy could drive one of these to work without blowing the budget, or take it to the local sanctioned strip without blowing his image. That's not an easy combination to come by these days.

Challenger R/T. Even on regular gas, it's quicker than the average bear. A few words for the hearty ... 340, 440 SixPack, Hemi. (See your Dealer.)

STANDARD EQUIPMENT

383 Magnum V8 (uses regular fuel) □ 3-speed manual fully synchronized with floor-mounted shift lever □ Vinyl front bucket seats with integral head restraints □ Simulated wood-grained door inserts □ Rallye Instrument Cluster—includes 8,000-rpm tach, 150-mph speedometer, trip odometer with push-button reset, oil pressure gauge, clock, and simulated wood-grained trim and steering wheel □ Dual exhausts □ F70x14 wide-tread, white sidewall, bias-belted tires □ Rallye Suspension Package (includes heavy-duty torsion bars, heavy-duty rear springs, and front sway bar) □ Rear sway bar □ Performance hood with detachable plates □ Brakes: 11" x 3", front; 11" x 2½", rear.

Now only available as a two-door hardtop, in 1971 the Challenger R/T was in its final year, although continued to be the high-performance model. Side stripes, R/T stickers and a blacked-out grille were the visible differences to base line models. A 383in³ V8, Rallye suspension, simulated wood grain trim, full Rallye instrument cluster and heavy-duty drum brakes completed the package.

CHALLENGER T/A
End of the road for the Do-It-Yourself Kit.

This is one car where the list of standard equipment is longer than the list of options. Hey, man, this isn't the beginning of something great, it's the grand finale.

The low-belted skins in front, big gar skins in back. This good crumb. Hard style. Power shag up front, drums, heavy-duty, in the rear. Dual exhausts with low-restriction mufflers, chrome side exit megaphones.

Challenger T/A. Just the way you'd do it yourself if you had the time. And the money. Yeah, the money. Frankly, it would probably cost you more to do it yourself. So why bother with do-it-yourself dreams? Check out this bargain for the man who'd rather be moving than building.

Check out the Standard Equipment List carefully. You'll find that everything is in order. From engine to drive train, Dodge puts it all together for you.

STANDARD EQUIPMENT

340 4-bbl. V8 □ TorqueFlite automatic transmission or 4-on-the-floor fully synchronized manual transmission. Fiber glass hood with fresh Air Pack □ Hood pins □ Special Rallye Suspension (includes rear sway bar, larger front sway bar, heavy-duty shock absorbers, increased camber of rear springs) □ Rear dust fan □ Low-restriction dual pipe and exhaust with megaphones □ Tires: E60x15, front; G60x15, rear; raised white letters □ 15x7.0JJ wheels □ Power front disc brakes with special semimetallic pads: 10" rear drums □ 3.55 axle ratio—8½" ring gear □ Vinyl front bucket seats □ Deep pile carpeting □ Simulated wood-grained door inserts □ Locking flip-top gas cap □ Flush outside door handles □ Body side tape stripes □ Grille and rock panel blackout.

The TA was still around and had a very impressive equipment list as standard, including a 340in³ V8 fitted with a 4-barrel carb, glassfiber hood with air scoop and hood pins, Rallye suspension pack which had front and rear sway bars, heavy-duty shocks, increased camber to rear springs and power front discs, to name just a few items.

When NASCAR boss Bill France plucked the aero warriors' feathers at the end of the 1970 season, the drivers went back to using almost stock Chargers. This is Buddy Arrington (no 5) during a pit-stop at the Daytona 500, being scrutinized by a NASCAR Winston Cup official.

the 300bhp 383, 440 Six-Pak and the 426 Hemi.

Sadly, this would be the last season that the mighty 426 Hemi would be readily available in either street or race guise until the 1990s, when Chrysler released a 'Crate-Hemi'. They say that imitation is the sincerest form of flattery, and the Hemi has been very flattered in its time. Other smaller manufacturers like Keith Black and Donovan have copied the engine almost exactly for racing purposes, but cast in lighter aluminum.

The Challenger, in only its second year, got a mild facelift, consisting of minor trim changes and fresh front and rear lights and grille. Surprisingly perhaps, the standard engine was still the slant six, but by far the most popular choice was the V8. Standard power plant for the single model R/T series was the 383in³ with the 426 Hemi and 440 Magnum available at extra cost. Challengers had the only convertible in the whole Dodge range and it was one of these convertibles that paced the 55th Indy 500. Although it was a beautiful pace car it has generally been forgotten, which is just how Dodge would like it kept, because it was this pace car that lost control while trying to exit the track and hit a group of spectators, killing one and seriously injuring others. Except for this tragic incident, 1971 was a good year for Dodge, with sales taking it up to 6th place in the manufacturer's league.

Some of that sales success may have something to do with the film released that year called *Vanishing Point*. Actor Barry Newman played Kowalski, a driver hired to take a white 440in³ powered 1970 Challenger hardtop from Colorado to California. The drug induced, psychedelic trip that ensued saw the main character storm across country, chased by the police, picking up gay hitchhikers, meeting a naked girl on a motorcycle and being guided by a blind radio jock called Supersoul, in what is regarded as one of the original road movies. The fiery climax sees Kowalski plough into a roadblock made up of bulldozers. Sharp-eyed moviegoers soon realized that it was not a Challenger that hit the roadblock. Chrysler had loaned Richard C. Sarafian, the director, five white 1970 Challengers and they wanted them back, so a derelict 1967 Chevrolet Camaro was purchased from a nearby junkyard and driven into the bulldozers. In 1997 the film was remade for TV, again starring a 1970 Challenger R/T, but this time fitted with the 426in^3 Hemi V8. The remake also featured a 1968 Charger driven by one of the cops.

NASCAR chief Bill France had been concerned about the high speeds that the modern race cars were obtaining. Laps of 200mph+ were great for spectators, but not for safety. It was because of this, more than any other reason, that the aero cars were limited to a maximum 305in^3 for the 1971 season, effectively killing the aero wars and making the Daytona and Superbird obsolete, although a Dodge Daytona did start the 1971 season. Driven by Richard (Dick) Brooks, the #22 winged car was fitted with a race ready, ultra short-stroke 305in^3 Hemi, and was entered for the Daytona 200. Brooks managed to take the car to the front until an accident caused some damage to the aerodynamics of the car that slowed it down considerably. He still managed to bring the Daytona home in 7th place and carried the honor of driving the last ever competitive race in a NASCAR series by a winged warrior, as he retired the car from racing straight after. Brooks and his Daytona were the exception to the rule – for the most part Mopar drivers had turned back to stock-bodied Chargers (and Plymouth Satellites).

Up against an impoverished Ford presence, Plymouth and Dodge walked away with the season. Ford drivers did win some Super speedway races, but Richard Petty in his baby blue '71 Satellite took 21 wins that year alone from the Plymouth total of 22, giving him the drivers' championship for the 3rd time. Dodge drivers picked up 8 wins to help ChryCo again take the manufacturers' title.

1970 Challenger. The star was plainly the car in this road movie as 'Kowalski' tries to win a bet, that he can deliver a car from Colorado to California in just 15hours. The makers had at their disposal five brand new white Challengers, four fitted with 440 magnum engines and one equipped with the standard 383ci V8. This last car was used for some interior shots. Although a little worse for wear, all five cars were returned to Chrysler at the end of filming.

The last of the performance-oriented Coronets was gone by 1971. This 1972 model, although still quite sporty-looking, even for a four-door, foretold the future for Dodge. As fuel-emission controls got tighter and insurance costs rose, horsepower dropped. Engines were either the frugal 225bhp slant-six or the 318in³ V8, which had now been reduced to 150bhp from the previous year's 230bhp. Coronets would get larger but weaker before being dropped at the end of 1976.

Although not quite dead, performance cars were becoming unfashionable by 1972. The move to unleaded petrol caused major de-tuning and lower compression ratios for all makers. Smaller cars continued to grow in popularity. Even so, Dodge still made some great hot cars. The Dart Demon was one of them. Facelifted from the 1971 model, the mover was still the Demon 340, which went virtually unchanged. The same 340in³ V8 was used but horsepower had shrunk from 275 to 240.

The Charger models took a major performance knock that

year. Both the R/T and SuperBee were dropped, along with the 500 series. A new Charger Rallye took up the performance torch for the intermediate size cars. Big block engines were dying fast. The 440 Six-Pak could still be had, but only as an option within the Rallye package, although a new 400in³ V8 was taking over throughout the Corporation. Whereas the Charger got only a mild front grille and rear light makeover, the Challenger was all-new. The new styling did look very much like the older car's but had a far more aggressive front

grille. Again, the R/T was dropped in favor of a new 'Rallye' hardtop. The beautiful Challenger convertible was also dropped and would be the last ChryCo convertible made until 1983. Dodge did continue to make 'big' cars, though. The Polara and Monaco were still in there and would soon be the only place to find a big block Dodge engine.

Back at the 'roundy-round' tracks, downsizing was forced home. NASCAR rules allowed use of Hemi motors but with carburetor specifications that were ineffective with the big block motors. The Hemi

With a continued move towards smaller cars, the Dodge Darts remained a popular choice. Keeping to a winning formula, the Dart went virtually unchanged for 1972. The Demon (front) and slightly longer Dart Swinger stayed as the performers. The base V8 was the 150bhp 318in³ motor except on the Demon 340, with the 240bhp 340in³ V8 optional on all other Darts.

The '72 Challengers underwent a complete body change but still looked very similar to the '71 models. With the demise of the convertible and R/T models, only two Challengers remained; the base Challenger and sportier Rallye, both two-door hardtops. No big blocks were available on any Challenger. The largest engine was the 340, rated at 240bhp.

It seemed to be the end of the line for true muscle cars. This 1972 Challenger Rallye (left) and Charger Rallye carried a dying performance torch. Both cars still looked mean and fast, but were gradually changing from high-performance vehicles into personal luxury sports cars; a different market.

would soon fade away from the racetrack along with the big wedge motors. The Grand National series was now sponsored by Winston tobacco company, and would soon change its name to the Winston Cup. Old rivals Chevrolet had returned to take Ford's place on the grid. Dodge had some success in 1972. Richard Petty fielded a Dodge

Charger as well as his Satellite in his last ever season for Plymouth. Alternating between the two cars, Petty picked up 7 wins (all in the Plymouth) and some 2nd place finishes (in the Charger) to take the championship for the 4th time. Bobby Isaac was still driving Chargers and won the Carolina 500 with Buddy Baker winning both the

This 1972 Charger SE was the most luxurious model in the single series line-up. New for '72 was a formal vinyl roof on the unique SE upper body. No R/T or SuperBee models were offered and both were replaced with a weaker Rallye model.

For the 1972 season, Dodge ace Buddy Baker was also driving a Petty Engineering car. He made super speedway history when he led the last thirty laps of the gruelling World 600 at Charlotte, North Carolina, to take the winner's flag in his no 11 Dodge Charger. He also won the Texas 500 later in the season. The Baker and Petty Chargers would go on to dominate the 1973 season, too.

This would be the last year that 'King' Richard Petty (no 43) would campaign a Plymouth. Later in the 1972 season he switched over to Dodge. This pit-stop shot shows Petty's nearly stock Road Runner. NASCAR rulings allowed only a certain number of pit crew near the cars, hence the long extensions on the cleaning equipment. Richard Petty took the car to eight Grand National wins.

Same pit crew, different car. By the end of the 1972 season, Richard Petty had changed entirely to the Dodge Charger and remained with Dodge until late 1978. Petty fondly remembers the '72 Charger as his all-time favorite stock car. With his eight Plymouth wins and twenty-five Dodge and Plymouth top 5 finishes, he won the Grand National championship.

As the '70s went on, it became increasingly difficult to find a performance car within Chrysler's ranks. However, the nimble little Dodge Dart remained. Formerly the Demon 340, it was now named the Sport 360. The larger 360in³ V8 with its two-barrel carb put out a respectable 245bhp. Power front disc brakes, sports suspension and shock absorbers, and a three-speed manual gearbox with floor-mounted stick shift were all part of the high-performance package. But with the consequences of the OPEC oil embargo of '73 still being felt, performance was a dirty word and only 3951 Sport 360s were sold.

World 600 at Charlotte, and the last race of the season, the Texas 500, in two different Chargers. Ex-Daytona driver Ray Elder also picked up a win. As a side note, country & western star Marty Robbins also campaigned a Dodge Charger in 1972, but with little success.

In 1973 OPEC imposed an oil embargo which almost immediately led to severe fuel shortages. The US Government was also imposing stronger emission controls, further strangling already decreasing performance levels. Through the rest of the seventies, Dodge continued to de-tune its engines until there were no real performance options left, and again went back to relying on its mechanical dependability and superior engineering to help sell cars. Due to complaints from religious groups, the compact Demon was renamed the Dart Sport 340. The Charger would receive weaker engines until its re-style in 1975 as a slab-sided monster,

The Dodge Challenger went mainly unchanged for 1973 except for its revised grille insert and large, unflattering black rubber bumper guards, which were necessary to meet safety regulations. The series kept two models: the base Challenger and Challenger Rallye, seen here in this period advert. The slant-six was dropped, leaving the 318in³ V8 as standard and the 340in³ V8 as the only upgrade.

The Charger also went pretty much unchanged for 1973. The main exception to this was a revised rear quarter window area, which had a far more conservative look to it and took away the car's aggressive edge. There were also new taillights. Available as a two-door coupé or two-door hardtop this year, the Charger remained popular until its demise at the end of 1978, but continued as just a shadow of its former self.

and its eventual demise in 1978. The Challenger went the same way, although it was dropped completely in 1974. The only flicker of performance through the mid to late seventies was the Dart replacement, the Aspen, which was not a bad looking little coupé and could be had in R/T form. The biggest engine was a mild 360in³ V8 which gave a mere 195bhp.

At the track, Petty had signed with Dodge for the '73 season and got off to a slow start, but won the championship in 1974 and '75 in his Dodge STP Charger. Dodge took the manufacturer's title in 1975. The K&K Insurance Charger was still winning, with driver Dave Marcis at the wheel. Petty would stay with Mopar until 1978 when after trying to race the Dodge Magnum he gave up on a hopeless task and signed up with Chevrolet. Dodge's last NASCAR win from this period came in 1977 when Neil Bonnet won the final race of that season, the LA Times 500. Dodge Division wouldn't see the inside of a

The '74 Challenger was identical to the '73 model. The Rallye package remained the best performer and with the end of the 340 V8 production, a larger 360in³ V8 was made available. The Rallye again came with fake side vents and performance hood with functional air scoops. Falling sales led to production being halted in early June 1975 with a total of just 16,437 completed.

NASCAR winners circle for another 20 years. Kyle Petty, Richard's son, did take one of Richards old Magnums to a win in his competitive debut when he took the checkered flag at the ARCA race, Daytona in 1979.

Throughout the late seventies and early eighties, Dodge cars were still entered in NASCAR races. But with no factory backing and brick-shaped vehicles, it became increasingly difficult to stay competitive. Finally, in June 1985, the last Dodge car ran in a NASCAR competition, driven by Phil Good at Pocono. Out of 40 starters he came in 30th. The drag strip remained the place to see Dodge in action. Dodge-powered altereds, top fuel dragsters and funny cars kept the Dodge flag flying.

The lean times of the late seventies for the Chrysler Corporation are now well documented, but a new Chairman in Lee Iacocca, a large loan from the US Government and the fresh front-wheel-drive K-cars, brought the company back from the brink of financial disaster. From the first few years of the eighties, Chrysler found itself sitting on a more stable corporate platform

King of the drag strip, Don 'Big Daddy' Garlits, now with a rear-engined dragster, won the 1975 NHRA and IHRA world championships. This Keith Black-built Dodge Hemi was sized at 480in³, taking the car to speeds of over 250mph and runs of 5.63 seconds.

and in a healthier economic climate, and so began a slow turn around towards performance vehicles. By 1984, Dodge had decided to market some new sports cars.

The highlight of the early eighties was the sub-compact Dodge Omni 024, which was a sporty coupé model of the base 4-door hatchback. These were made in De Tomaso, GLH (Goes Like Hell), GLH-S (Goes Like Hell-Somemore) and Shelby versions. They were produced between 1979 and 1987. Based upon the stubby European Talbot Horizon, good-looking they certainly

were not – but when fitted with a longer, more streamlined coupé body and a Turbo-charged engine, these nimble little cars could make 0-60 in around 7 seconds.

Mid-1976 saw the introduction of the Dart replacement, the Aspen. Available as a sedan, station wagon or a 2-door coupé, initial sales were brisk, reaching 219,449 units, by far Dodge's best-seller that year. Either a frugal but reliable 225in^3 slant-six or a 318in^3 V8 powered the Aspen as standard, although a 360in^3 V8 was on the options list. The Aspen utilized a new transverse torsion

Don Garlits in 1999, standing outside his Museum of Drag Racing with one of his early front-engined top fuel dragsters. It was a configuration like this that almost cost Don his life when an engine exploded in his face. After recovering from the accident, he went on to devise the rear-engined racer and campaigned for safer guidelines.

bar suspension up front instead of the more traditional longitudinal bars, supposedly offering that 'big car ride' in a compact vehicle. Of the three body styles, the semi-fastback SE trim level coupé was the performance pick of the crop. Sitting on a shorter (108.5in) wheelbase than the sedan and wagon, the 2-door came with a 60/40 split seat, dual recliners, a central armrest and a formal landau roof with opera windows. From 1976 through to 1980, (when the Aspen was replaced by the Aries) the coupé was available with an R/T package, which could be beefed up even further with a Super Pak option.

The De Tomaso package was launched in 1980 and was advertised as 'The Italian sports car from Detroit.' Essentially this was a dress-up kit for the Dodge 024 coupé. With input from Alejandro De Tomaso of Italy, the vehicle featured a front air dam, rear spoiler, fender flares,

1978 Aspen R/T. The R/T option was just one of three suspension and trim packages available, along with the super coupé and the Aspen street kit coupé that went to make up Dodge's 'Street Fleet'. The R/T came in either black or white paint, set off by dramatic red, orange and yellow striping along the rear, sides and hood. This was matched with large R/T decals, front and rear spoilers, rear quarter window louvers, flared wheelarches, side mouldings and painted sports mirrors. Underneath the car was a heavy-duty suspension, FR78x14 GBR black walls tires wrapping around Rallye wheels, and a 360in³ V8 from the options list. On the street, the car was hard to miss ...

louvered rear windows, brushed metal roof 'band', cast aluminum 'deep-dish' 13in wheels fitted with wide P185/70R13 tires, De Tomaso decals on the fuselage and a special sport suspension. Only two body colors were available – graphic red and bright yellow, with black accents. The interior featured black vinyl bucket seats, Rallye instrument cluster, floor

mats with the De Tomaso logo, a special dash plaque and a leather wrapped steering wheel and shift knob. The power plant was a 1.7-liter in-line four VW engine, matched to a 4-speed manual gearbox.

The Dodge Hamtramck plant sits in a suburb of Detroit, Michigan, and has grown even more since this picture was taken in the early 1980s. Parts of the plant date back to the original 1914 factory.

For 1981 the De Tomaso changed very little, except the car now sat on 14in wheels, had a new color option of silver and came with the newly introduced 2.2-liter Chrysler in-line four. Sales dropped from 1333 in 1980 to just 619 in 1981. This was the last year of the Dodge De Tomaso package, but sales were good for the new Charger 2.2 option (7306 units), which developed into a series all its own the following year.

In 1983 the 024 designation was gone completely, and all Omni-based coupes were named Charger. Mid-1983 saw the introduction of the Shelby Charger. Carroll Shelby is of course famous for his exploits as a racing driver and builder of performance engines and cars, most notably the Cobra and Mustang, and whilst working with Ford became close friends with the then Ford boss, Lee Iacocca. When Iacocca moved to Chrysler on 2 November 1978 as president, his friendship with Shelby went along too, so it was really only a matter of time before Shelby was offered the chance to cast his magic performance wand over some Chrysler vehicles. Carroll dictated a large number of changes to the base Charger. In Shelby's own

words, "I laid out all the parameters that I wanted in the car. The main parameters were to have as good a handling front-wheel-drive car as there is anywhere, that it be unique in appearance, and that it perform adequately." The performance turned out to be more than adequate.

To squeeze 107bhp out of the 2.2-liter instead of the regular 94bhp, the people at Shelby boost

Based on the Dodge Omni, the Charger received the Carroll Shelby touch. First introduced in 1983, by 1985 the Shelby Charger had received a turbo-charged 135in³ in-line four that gave out an impressive 146bhp. For such a small car, that was power aplenty.

By 1986 the K-car-based Daytona was in its third year and was more refined. The Turbo Z was aimed directly at the younger, performance-minded buyer. The fastback coupé had a unique body kit and could be supplied with a C/S (Carroll Shelby) performance package. A removable glass T-top was new for '86.

DODGE SHELBY CHARGER
5/50 PROTECTION. STANDARD

Ma'am?
We felt obliged to bring you up to, uhm, speed about this "arrangement" we made with your little boy, Carroll.

Doubtless you recollect him asking if he could do some "fixin'" on one of Dodge's perfectly respectable Chargers? How he got to messin' around with its suspension and such – bigger brakes, gas shocks, rear sway bar, lower center of gravity, and super sticky Goodyear Eagle GTs on cheese-grater wheels. How he even slapped racing stripes on it and stitched up some new-fangled custom interior?

And I trust you'll also recall what he did to the engine. Took our optional 2.2 OHC and bolted a danged turbocharger on it. A water-

MRS. SHELBY, YOUR SON'S BEEN ACTING UP AGAIN.

cooled one at that! (Thing's quicker'n a buckin' horse through the gate," he freely admits.)

Miz Shelby? This here car of Carroll's ain't nothin' but some kind of new wave, high tech hot rod. Can you imagine the wringer he put us through trying to blanket this Shelby Charger with our famous 5/50 Protection Plan?* But we did. Well, as if all that

hasn't been enough, ma'am, do you know what your youngster is up to now? Actin' up, that's what. He's got himself a bunch of ol' boys racing that feisty little hot rod. And they're winning!

Anyhow, we just thought you should know, ma'am how absolutely delighted we all are. Especially since we also found a way to hang a tag of just $9315† on the whole enchilada.

PS. Miz Shelby, you know how much we think of young Carroll, but do you suppose you could have a word or two with him 'bout settin' down a bit? I mean, just long enough so we can all catch our breath.

Dodge
DIVISION OF CHRYSLER CORPORATION

AN AMERICAN REVOLUTION

*5 year or 50,000 mile limited warranty on powertrain and outer body rust through. Restrictions apply. Excludes leases. See copy at dealer. †Sticker price excludes tax and destination charges. Price may change after printing. See dealer for latest information.   BUCKLE UP FOR SAFETY.

1987 Dodge Shelby Charger. One of the few real performance cars from the Chrysler stables, the Shelby Charger was a limited production run of the successful standard Omni Charger. Not just a paint job and nice interior, the Shelby version had boosted compression to 9.6, a warmer overhead cam that was retarded 4 degrees, tuned exhaust, larger brakes, gas shock absorbers, Eagle GT tires fitted on unique wheels, and a turbo charger. This was one fast car. In its last year of production, 2011 units were built, but the final 1000 were purchased by Shelby himself and became the very limited 1987 Charger GLHS.

compression to 9.6, and fitted a warmer overhead cam (retarded four degrees for better top-end performance) and a tuned exhaust. The engine was then mated to a 5-speed manual gearbox. Fitted with this setup the car went from 0-60 in 9.0 seconds and had a 16.8 second ET at 82mph; top speed was 117mph.

The cars came in either Santa Fe Blue or Radiant Silver with a very wide contrasting silver or blue center stripe and had a blanked out rear quarter panel, front air dam, stiffer sports suspension, larger tires, larger disc brakes at the front, larger drums on the back and unique CS interior trim and decals all as standard. Fun to drive and with a price tag of nearly $2000 more than the standard coupé, which retailed at $6379, they were still well received with more than 8000 of these speciality sports cars being made that year.

Shelby also suggested to Iacocca that they should try something with the mundane Omni 4-door and in 1984 Dodge released the Omni GLH. The GLH name tag, also suggested by Shelby, stood for Goes Like Hell, which it did, and these little cars could do 0 to 60 in just 8.5 seconds. After more development, a GLH-S (Goes Like Hell-Somemore) was produced in 1986.

As for the Shelby Charger, 1984 saw the appearance of a Torqueflite automatic gearbox to the options list, but this only stayed for one season and was dropped again. The next big development was the addition of turbo power in 1985. The standard 110bhp 2.2 Charger engine was now able to produce a whopping 146bhp when turbocharged, could get to 60mph in 7.8 seconds and achieve a top speed of 124mph. This year also saw another paint combination, black with a silver stripe.

It is important to note that while Dodge was producing the Charger models, it was also making the Hi-Po K-car-based Daytona coupé and then later the Shadow and as sales improved with the Daytona, sales of the Charger gradually started to fall.

In 1987, the Charger's final year, only 1011 Shelbys were ordered, against 24,275 regular Chargers, 33,104 Daytona's and 76,056 Shadows, these last being the direct replacement for the now dated Omni line, so in March 1987 all Charger production ceased. In fact, total production was actually 2011 but the last 1000 were bought by Carroll Shelby and they would become the 87 Charger GLHSs.

In terms of style, the Shelby Chargers went virtually unchanged from year to year. In 1985 a speed hump appeared on the hood to allow room for the turbo, adding to the side-sill ground-effect spoilers and unique rear deck spoiler from the previous year. Chargers also had single deep-set square headlamps opposed to the standard quad setup. An option from 1985 that became standard in its final year was a large fully removable tinted glass sunroof complete with vinyl storage bag. 1986 was basically a carryover year; the only significant change was the addition of a third brake light, mounted in the center of the spoiler, in deference to federal regulations.

The Charger was one name that was resurrected, but it wasn't the only one. The new Daytona arrived in 1984 sitting on a modified K-car chassis and used a 2.2-liter transverse four, but that's just about where the similarities ended between the Daytonas and the rest of the boxy K-cars. They were all 2-door sports coupes of a 'fast-hatch' style. Between 1984 and 1993, the Daytona's hottest derivations were the 'Z', Shelby and IROC R/T, with the Daytona Shelby Z being arguably the best of the bunch.

1996 saw the introduction of a pure race version of the Viper, the GTS-R (racing). The French-run Oreca team used a factory-backed GTS-R and had a shakedown year in the FIA GT1 race series, but was plagued by teething troubles. The following year a move to the GT2 series brought more success.

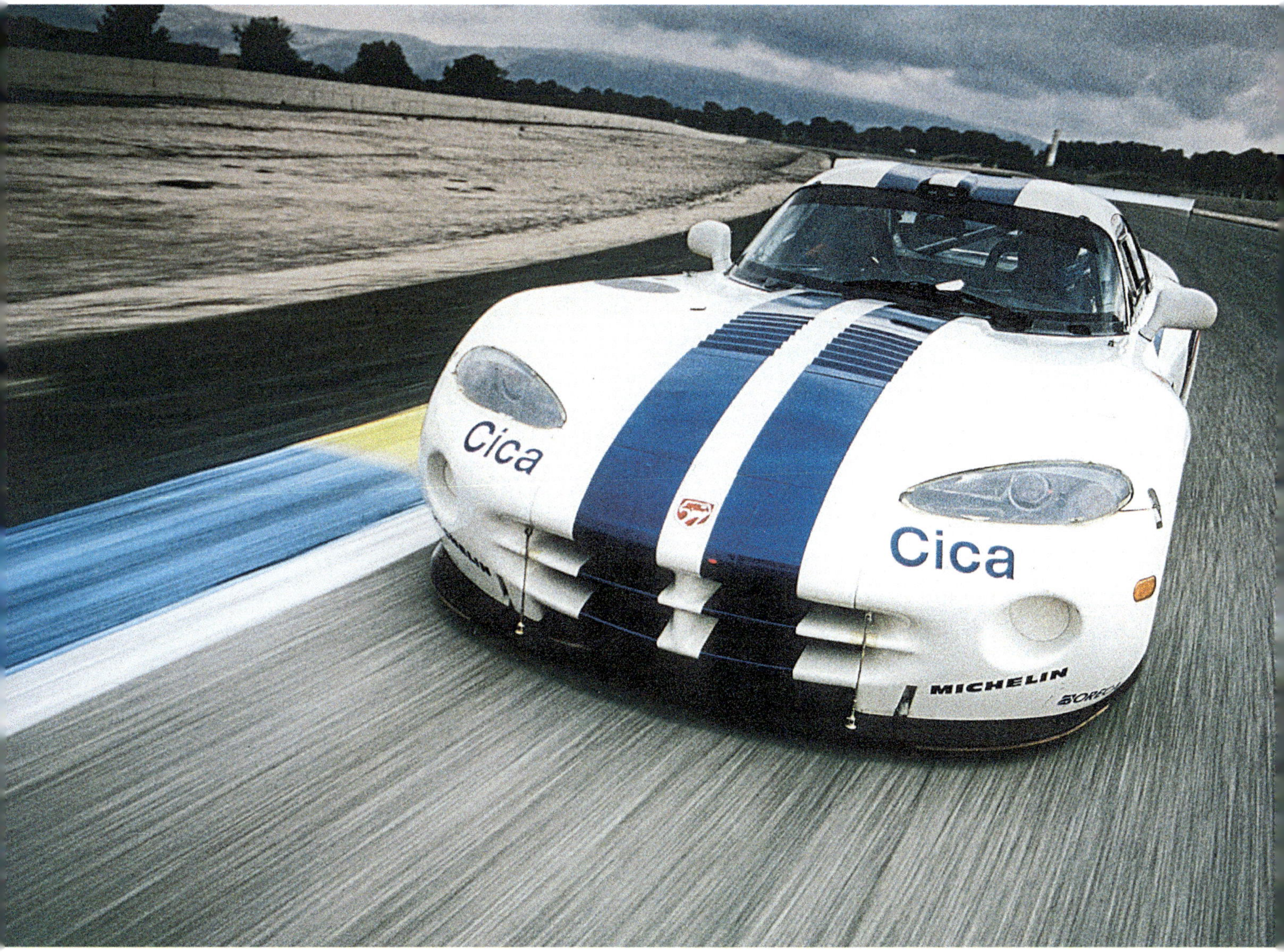

DODGE FINDS A VIPER'S NEST

In 1991, Dodge released the super slick Stealth. Although often compared to sports cars, the Dodge Stealth was a grand touring 2+2 sport coupé. It was largely based on the 1988 Intrepid concept car and shared a wheelbase platform with other Chrysler divisions of 97.2in, but the Stealth carried a larger body. Very European in styling, the body was designed by Tom Gale's team at Chrysler, but built at the Chrysler-Mitsubishi plant in Illinois and Nagoya, Japan, utilizing Mitsubishi mechanics. Mitsubishi sold the car as a GTO in Europe or 3000GT in the United States.

The Stealth was available in four models, each fitted with a V6. The base model used a 164hp version that had a twin valve per cylinder setup, but the ES and R/T

1991 Stealth R/T. With the introduction of the Stealth, nobody could doubt that Dodge was back in the performance car business. Available as a base, ES and this R/T version, all cars were front-wheel drive with the ES and R/T variants using a double overhead cam 181in³ V6 that gave 222bhp and a top speed of 160mph.

models had a double overhead cam and four valves per cylinder that kicked out 222hp. Pick of the pack was the R/T Turbo, which added a pair of intercooled Turbochargers that was good for 300bhp and 160mph+. The car was an important statement from Dodge that this division was back in the performance business, in a big way. The Stealth wowed the performance-starved Mopar fan, but what was to come next would bowl

them over completely – the Dodge Viper production car.

On 4 January 1989, the Viper RT/10 concept made its world debut at the North American International Auto Show in Detroit. Although Chrysler execs knew they had something special, they were not expecting the overwhelming response that came from the public. People were cueing up to offer deposits for a production car that did not exist.

A decision to develop the roadster was taken and a handpicked team of around seventy car-crazy engineers and designers set to work within a 'platform team' to test the viability of turning this concept into a full production car.

Working closely with major parts manufacturers, the team, headed by Roy H Sjoberg, developed unique components that could not only withstand the extreme stresses of

1992 Viper V10 engine. The new Viper RT/10 came with an new all-aluminum 90 degree V10 engine – an OHV 8-liter (488in³) lightweight powerplant with twenty valves, roller-type hydraulic lifters and forged steel connecting rods and crankshaft. With a compression ratio of 9.6:1, it gave out 490lb/ft of torque at 3700rpm. Fuel delivery was through a sequential multi-port electronic fuel-injection system.

Introduced in early 1992, the Viper RT/10 was almost unchanged from the 1989 concept car. This powerful open roadster came with a 488in³ aluminum V10 engine that put out a hefty 400bhp. Fewer than 200 were built in its first year, but production would jump to 1043 in 1993. A pre-production Viper RT/10 paced the seventy-fifth Indy 500 race in May 1991.

a powerful performance car but which also enhanced the RT/10's capabilities. In May of 1990, the Viper got the big 'GO' from Chrysler boss Bob Lutz. Pre-production publicity got a major boost when a very early prototype RT/10 received the honor of pacing the Indy 500 race in May of '91, and in December of 1991, the very first production Vipers rolled off the line as 1992 models.

The New Mack Avenue assembly plant was like no other that Chrysler had at the time. 'Production line' isn't the correct way to describe the plant. Each car was hand-built by a team of 120 skilled craftspeople at a series of workstations, each individual being their own inspectors. The production model was amazingly close to the original concept. A 488in³ (8-liter) aluminum V10 remained as the power-plant of the all-red two seat open top roadster. Only 162 were made in the remaining months of that model year. All sold immediately, some going for far more than the

$50,000 factory price. It became an instant classic, and by 1994 had even spawned a TV film and series, called simply *Viper*.

Set slightly in the future, it featured a morphing RT/10 police car that turned into a weapon-laden silver car called the Defender. This was designed by Chrysler stylist Steve Ferrerio with input from the filmmakers. The show also highlighted a host of Chrysler concept vehicles including the Dodge Stealth, Plymouth Slingshot, Chrysler Portofino, Chrysler Epic Minivan, and Caravan III.

The following year saw production leap to just over 1000 cars at New Mack. Specifications went unchanged, but they could now also be ordered in black.

Also back in 1991, Chrysler introduced the Spirit R/T. Styled like a house brick, it was however powered by a version of the 2.2-liter K-car engine fitted with a 16-valve DOHC head designed by Lotus. Fed by a Garrett Systems

intercooled turbocharger, this Turbo III engine produced 224hp. The R/T also featured unique interior and exterior trim to set itself apart from other Spirits. The only available transmission in the R/T was a heavy-duty A568 5-speed manual transmission built by Chrysler's New Process Gear Division located in Syracuse, New York. Heavy-duty vented disc brakes all around came as standard, with optional anti-lock brakes. Color-keyed 15 in alloy wheels were standard, fitted with P205/60R15 tires.

At the time, the R/T was advertised as "the fastest sedan made in America", with Chrysler rating its performance above BMWs M5. It could hit 60mph in 5.8 seconds, according to *Car and Driver*, making it one of the quickest front-wheel-drive cars ever offered in the American market. It was chosen as *Motor Trend* magazine's "Domestic Sport Sedan of the Year", beating the Ford Taurus SHO for 1991 and 1992.

CHRYSLER RETAKES STYLING LEADERSHIP

The resurgence of Chrysler as a styling leader in the early Nineties took everyone by surprise. Thomas C Gale, head of design at Chrysler, is generally accepted as being the man responsible for getting the Corporation back at the top in the design stakes. The fresh and distinctive 'cab-forward' styling that typified the 1990's corporate line-up made Chrysler's future much more secure, even before the Daimler takeover. For 1993, Dodge's first 'Cab-forward' LH cars were released. The Intrepid was low, swift and an instant success. A choice of two V6 engines at either 201in^3 or 215in^3 and horsepower ratings of 153 or 214bhp respectively, gave them an excellent power to weight ratio. Optional performance suspension, all-round discs and 16in wheels helped make the ES version the sensible choice for comfortable touring with power on tap.

Although officially a 1995 model, the new Neon was released early in 1994 as part of the build-up to

1993 Intrepid. The Intrepid was the Dodge version of the new-generation LH cars. Technically advanced and very modern-looking, the base car was aimed more at the family buyer with the ES version (left) being the performance option. Standard fare on the ES included front bucket seats, all-round disc brakes, 16in touring tires and a 214bhp 215in^3 V6, with sports suspension as an option. The LH sedan bodies were shared throughout the corporation. Chrysler's Concorde and Eagle's Vision were of the same 'cab-forward' design and all were available with dual airbags, traction control, anti-lock brakes and a choice of two V6 engines. The ES came with the 3.5-liter, double overhead cam 24 valve version of the V6.

The Neon was introduced in early 1994 and was a smaller version of the 'cab-forward' LH sedans. It soon earned a name for fun motoring. The Neon was made available with a sports ACR package and had its own racing series. This unique sports package included a new 2-liter 16-valve engine that gave 132bhp and did 0–60 in less than 8 seconds, all-round disc brakes, 1436 alloy wheels with 175/65 Goodyear tires, a specially rated steering box, larger radiator, and sports suspension with front and rear anti-roll bars.

Dodge campaigned the Neon in SCCA and also found favor with amateur racers in Solo I and Solo II classes. Chrysler President Bob Lutz is pictured here with the Neon Speedster that he drove in the Neon Challenge at the Detroit Grand Prix.

Now with its own sport division, Dodge was well and truly back in motorsport. One of its most successful vehicles was the Dakota pick-up truck. Dodge Motorsport-backed teams entered the NASCAR Craftsman Truck series and also ran in the NHRA. This is Team Mopar driver Scott Patterson in his NHRA Pro Stock Truck class Dakota dragster.

replace the Dodge Shadow. Based on a shorter version of the LH sedan's 'cab-forward' look, the Neon was available as a Dodge or Plymouth (and Chrysler in Europe). Another 4-door sedan, the Neon, while not a performance car in the true sense, would soon have its own racing series, together with an optional street performance (ACR) package list that would make this car a real mover. However, while at first appearing to be a nice styling touch, the frameless front door windows soon became a troublesome thorn in most owners' sides. Excessive wind noise, jams and falling glass all became prevalent, but the most common fault reported with the car was blown head gaskets, a problem shared with other Dodge vehicles at the time.

The initial base power unit was a 121in³ (2-liter) 4-cylinder that gave out 132bhp. Surprisingly, the Dodge

(Left) The 1995 Avenger was the 'cab-forward' replacement for the Daytona. Dodge Motorsport Division soon put the new car to work. This is Team Mopar driver Scott Geoffrion in his Dodge Avenger Pro Stock dragster.

1995 Neon. Just a year after its launch, Dodge introduced a 2-door version of its nippy Neon. Offered in either Highline or Sport trim, the coupé was available with a 150bhp DOHC version of the 2-liter tranverse-4 engine that sat neatly underneath the power-bulge hood. The coupé shared a host of standard equipment with its 4-door sister including power windows, twin airbags, anti-lock brakes and disc brakes all round. When it launched in the UK and Japan in 1996, it also came with electric folding wing mirrors and air-conditioning.

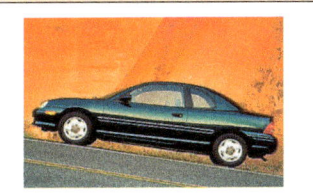

Neon outsold the supposedly more popular Plymouth version by nearly 2000 units in its first year. By '94, the Stealth ES had been dropped to leave just the base model, the R/T and the R/T Turbo. The R/T Turbo was given a 6-speed Getrag manual gearbox, while the base model and R/T kept the tried and tested 5-speed transmission. Also optional in these two models was a 4-speed automatic transmission, which featured driver controllable Power/Economy modes. Production had dropped from a high of 18,352 units in 1991 to just 7090 units in 1994.

The 1995 model year saw yet more introductions of all-new 'cab-forward' cars, as the sporty Avenger coupé and Stratus sedan were released. The Avenger replaced the now dated Daytona and left just the Shadow in its last season, as a reminder of eighties styling.

The Avenger and its close cousin, the Chrysler Sebring coupé, were designed by Chrysler but built by Mitsubishi in Illinois. They shared a modified Mitsubishi Galant platform. Sebrings and Avengers differed only in their front grille and taillights; however, Dodge's version came with fewer standard features but a lower price tag. The new 2-door sports coupé came with 152in^3 (2.5-liter) V6 as standard on the performance ES model.

Introduced early in 1995, the 4-door Stratus was a close cousin of the more luxury-oriented Chrysler Cirrus and the less expensive Plymouth Breeze sedans. Again, all three sported unique grilles and different taillights, but Stratus offered a wider engine selection than its stable mates. Marketed in base and ES trim, Stratus sedans came with standard antilock brakes and dual

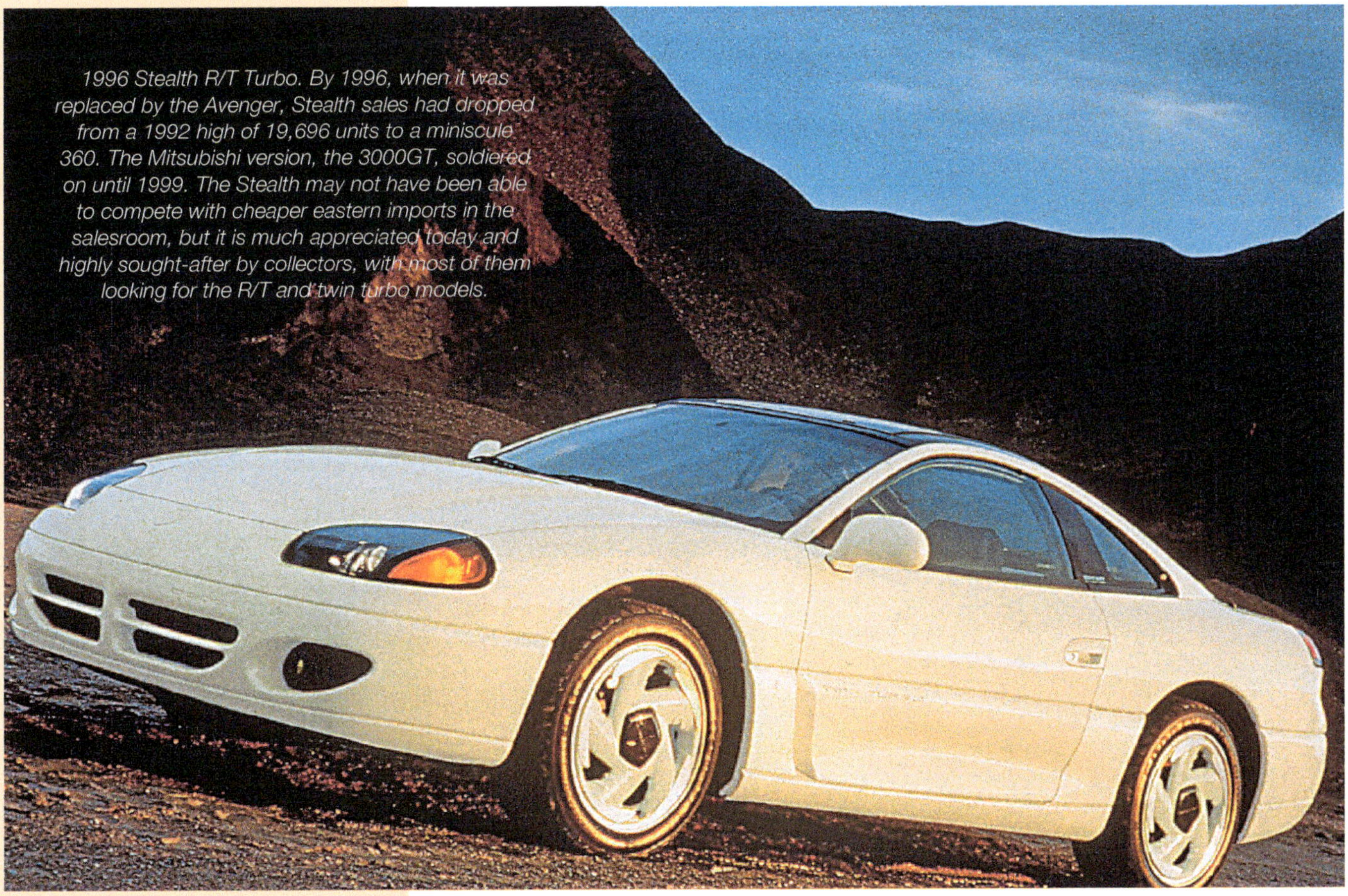

1996 Stealth R/T Turbo. By 1996, when it was replaced by the Avenger, Stealth sales had dropped from a 1992 high of 19,696 units to a miniscule 360. The Mitsubishi version, the 3000GT, soldiered on until 1999. The Stealth may not have been able to compete with cheaper eastern imports in the salesroom, but it is much appreciated today and highly sought-after by collectors, with most of them looking for the R/T and twin turbo models.

The Viper RT/10 received a power boost in 1996 when a rear-exit exhaust system replaced the side pipes, increasing output to 415bhp. A new 'double bubble' removable hardtop was put on the optional list, along with yellow wheels and decals.

1996 was a big year for the Viper. Having already achieved overwhelming popularity, the RT/10 received a sister in the form of a hardtop coupé, the GTS. Classed as a 1997 model, the sleek blue coupé received rave reviews and a rush of orders. The GTS design was inspired by a rich heritage of American grand touring performance cars. Vehicles like the Shelby Cobra Daytona and this Hemi-powered 1953 Cunningham C3 coupé (owned by ex-Chrysler CEO Bob Lutz) both donated styling and performance cues – the long nose and short rear deck, that aggressive stance. It exuded the impression of tremendous power waiting to be unleashed.

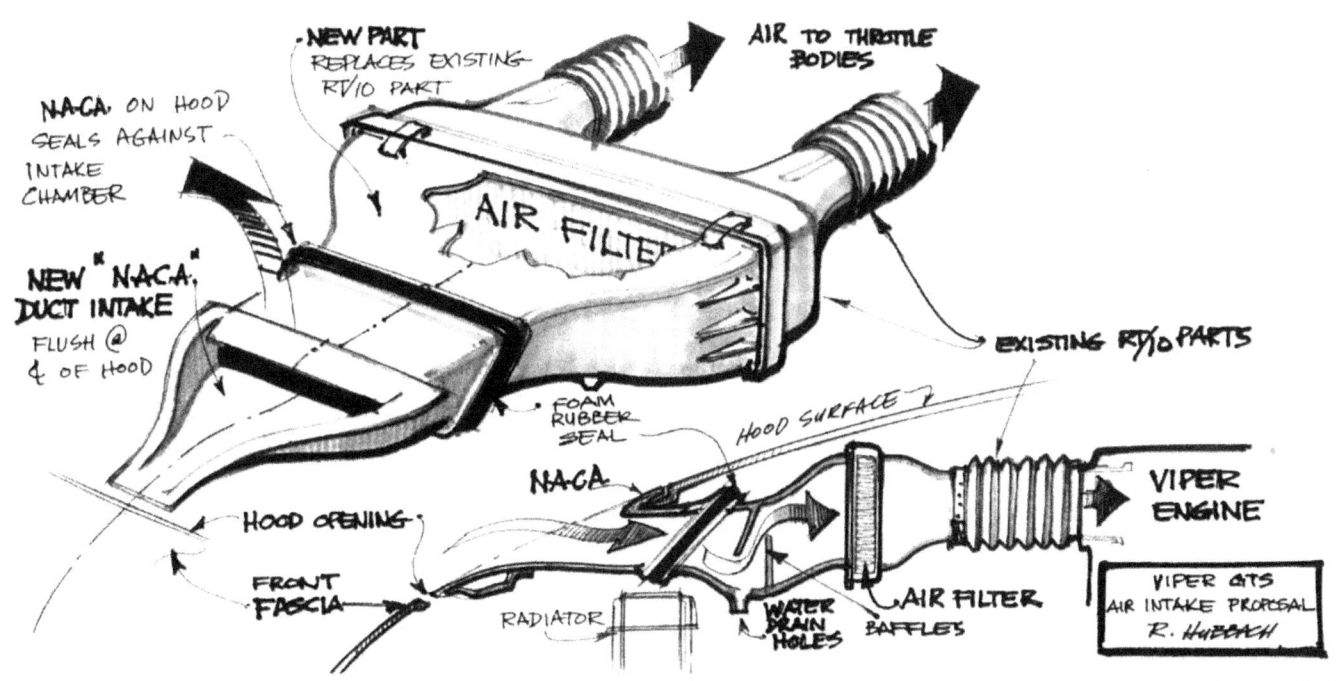

Labels on diagram:
- NACA ON HOOD SEALS AGAINST INTAKE CHAMBER
- NEW PART REPLACES EXISTING RT/10 PART
- AIR TO THROTTLE BODIES
- AIR FILTER
- NEW "NACA" DUCT INTAKE FLUSH @ ℄ OF HOOD
- EXISTING RT/10 PARTS
- FOAM RUBBER SEAL
- HOOD SURFACE
- NACA
- VIPER ENGINE
- HOOD OPENING
- FRONT FASCIA
- RADIATOR
- WATER DRAIN HOLES
- AIR FILTER BAFFLES
- VIPER GTS AIR INTAKE PROPOSAL R. HUBBACH

airbags. Base power train was a 132hp, 2.0-liter, 4-cylinder engine taken from the Neon, matched to a 5-speed manual transmission. Neons were now available as 2-door coupes, and could be had with a larger 150bhp twin-cam motor.

The Stealth was now in its final months of production, with the last few imports sold as 1996 models. They were virtually unchanged from the previous year although Mitsubishi's 3.0-liter DOHC twin turbocharged V6 was available on the R/T Turbo from '94 onward. This increased power from 300 to 320hp and offered a 0-60 time of just 5.3 seconds. Vipers again went unchanged except for the color choice, which for '95 included Bright Yellow and Emerald Green. Viper production was moved from the New Mack Assembly Plant to Conner Avenue in October 1995.

As the decade went in to its second half, things got more exciting at Dodge. For the 1996 season, Dodge exhibited the rear-engined Intrepid ESX show car – a look at how the next generation of Chrysler's LH

Aerodynamics played a large part in the development of the Viper GTS. This is an initial design rendering of the fully functional NACA duct in the center of the hood. The idea was borrowed from NASA and was designed to maximize air intake with minimum wind resistance. The design team achieved a coefficient of just 0.39.

Viper GTS frame. The RT/10 frame was improved upon for the GTS. Known already for being stiff on the roadster, the GTS frame, although 50lb lighter, managed to be stiffer still. The car has a backbone tubular space frame with a separate cowl structure, and accommodates cast-aluminum upper and lower 'A' arms, Koni coil-over-shock units and front and rear tubular stabilizer bars.

sedans would develop, along with being a test-bed for fuel saving ideas.

Switching back to production vehicles, the Neon went on sale in the UK and Japan badged as Chryslers but only with the SOHC engine.

Meanwhile, the American 4-door Neon could be had in sport trim and fitted with the optional DOHC engine. The Intrepid ES received as standard, the 214bhp 215in³ (3.5-liter) V6, while the Stratus, when fitted with

the optional Mitsubishi V6, could be equipped with Chrysler's 'Autostick' transmission, which permitted shifting up or down through the gears by tilting the shift lever left or right. Biggest news on the performance front was the introduction of a new Viper – a hardtop coupé called the GTS.

Built alongside the RT/10 at the new Conner Avenue Plant, the hardtop coupé was based very much on the 1993 Viper GTS show car. Overwhelming interest in that car soon led to the decision to build the coupé. The GTS, although looking very similar indeed to the RT/10 and mechanically just about the same, didn't share a single exterior body panel with its sister car. The GTS had a smaller aerodynamic grille

opening and extended lower lip; the long hood had a NACA intake with air louvers over the front wheels. Now that sounds familiar somehow; hmm ... what page was that Daytona on? The sloping twin bubble roof led to a 'hatch' style rear end that encompassed a built-in rear spoiler, which housed a neat Viper emblem in the center that doubled as a brake light.

A new second-generation 8-liter V10 engine got a redesigned lightweight aluminum cylinder block with permanent cast-iron cylinder liners. Along with lighter cylinder heads and the new rear-exit exhaust system, power was pumped up to 450hp and a torque rating of 490lb-ft @ 3700rpm, making the Viper the most powerful American

Once again a Viper was picked to pace the Indianapolis 500 motor race in 1996, and this time it was the new GTS coupé. Powered by a second-generation V10 engine, the GTS output had increased to 450bhp, with speeds in the 200mph region now achievable. A sporty Dodge Ram pick-up was chosen as the official truck for the race.

production car in history. The GTS, officially a 1997 model, far outstripped the RT/10 in production. For 1996, 1889 RT/10s were made, but the following year only 76 open roadsters were built compared to 1607 GTS. And once again, the Viper, this time the new GTS, paced the Indy 500, being driven by none other than Chrysler President at the time, Bob Lutz.

In 1995 Dodge released the Stratus, its version of the compact JA sedan. Launched as a 1996 model along with its Chrysler Cirrus twin, it offered comfortable 'intermediate-size' room in a compact package. First year sales were a promising 115,378. Dodge Motorsport Division used a race-prepped Stratus in the new North American Super Touring championship with some success. This is Dominic Dobson's no 7 car with PPG markings.

In the Super Touring championship's first year, Dodge driver David Donohue won the first race and finished third overall. The 1997 season brought even more success when he drove this Dodge-backed Infinity/Silicon Graphics no 8 Stratus and won the drivers' championship. Dodge withdrew from the series before the start of the next year.

BACK TO THE TRACK

It was in 1996 that Dodge finally got back into motorsport in a big way. Although regrettably not NASCAR stock cars, the new Stratus did represent Dodge in the new Super-Touring Sedan Series with some success, but it was Dodge pick-up trucks that made the biggest noise. The recently restyled Ram was entered in the NASCAR Craftsman Truck Series, and at the time of publication continued to run very successfully indeed ... but we had better stick to the cars – Dodge pick-ups are another story altogether. A factory-backed Viper GTS-R (racing) started to show its muscle

Sales of the new GTS far outweighed those of the RT/10. In its first full year of production 1607 coupes were built, compared to just 76 RT/10s. Public interest was stimulated when Chrysler CEO Bob Lutz, himself a one-time racing driver, took the wheel of the Indy 500 pace car. Here, Lutz gets directions for his final practice lap from a USAC official before the start of the eightieth running of the famous motor race.

The Oreca team had a better year in 1997. With all of the problems worked out, the team won the GT2 series and British driver Justin Bell took the drivers' championship. This is Justin Bell in his no 53 Viper during the gruelling 1997 Le Mans 24 hour race. He went on to take the checkered flag in the GT2 class.

when it was campaigned in the FIA GT1 world racing series. A rethink in strategy would see a change the following year when the car moved to the GT2 series, with far better results.

In terms of cars, 1997 was a relatively quiet year for Dodge. The Neons went unchanged and the Avenger and Stratus received very minor facelifts. The Copperhead concept car debuted as a baby Viper with rumours that it would go into production in the next millennium, but Dodge was concentrating on a new, fast growing market, the sports-utility, and although a fantastic looking car, it remained a concept. Its Ram and new smaller Ram-styled Dakota got more car-like, and sales boomed.

At the track David Donohue won the Super-Touring Drivers Championship in his Stratus. With

Dodge Motorsport Division wanting to concentrate on other kinds of racing, Dodge withdrew from Super-Touring immediately after, although the team cars, now in private hands, continued to win occasional races in a South American race series. The Viper GTS-R had an incredible year. British driver Justin Bell took his factory-backed #53 Viper to 10 podium places out of 11 races, including 3 wins, to take the GT2 World Championship.

In the spring of 1997 Dodge won its first NASCAR race in twenty years, finishing 1 and 2 in a Super-Truck series race – marking the return of a legend for Mopar fans as the famous 'Petty Blue' color with the #43 painted on the side came in second. Richard Petty was still going strong.

The 1998 Neons went unchanged but the R/T label made a

welcome return on the Neon coupé. Most of the features of the ACR (American Club Racer) cars were fitted, as well as Viper-like speed stripes along the length of the vehicle. The ACR program was introduced to allow buyers to get a race spec car direct from any dealer and drive it to the local track to compete in grassroots racing.

The Intrepid was all-new, and followed styling cues that could be directly traced back to 1986, when designer Kevin Verduyn completed the initial exterior design of a new aerodynamic concept sedan called Navajo. The design never passed the clay model stage but it was at this time that the Chrysler Corporation purchased bankrupt Italian manufacturer Lamborghini. The Navajo's exterior design was

1998 Top Fuel dragster. The drag strip has always been a second home for Dodge. Pro Stock, Funny Cars, Trucks and Top Fuel dragsters have all been powered by Dodge. This is Mike Dunn in the Team Mopar/Darrell Gwynn Top Fuel Dragster competing on the NHRA circuit. He finished fifth in the '98 point standings. More recently he lowered the NHRA Top Fuel national elapsed-time to 4.503 seconds.

Oreca wasn't the only team to race Vipers in '98. The British-based Chamberlain team has campaigned the GTS-R since 1997, and also entered two cars in the 1998 Le Mans race. They finished a respectable fifth and seventh position. During the 1999 FIA season the Chamberlain team usually managed to be in the top 5, and the Belmondo team (also running Vipers) beat the Oreca Vipers when they met at Homestead USA in September 1999.

reworked and became the (Chrysler) Lamborghini Portofino concept. The Portofino was heralded as a design triumph when it launched at the Frankfurt Auto Show in 1987, setting in motion Chrysler's decision to produce a production sedan with the Portofino's revolutionary design, called 'cab-forward'. The Intrepid and its corporate siblings stole styling leadership away from GM. The Intrepid ES was the performance option with alloy wheels, autostick transmission and a 225bhp 197in^3 (3.2-liter) V6.

A limited edition of 100 Viper GT2 road cars were built. All came with full race body kit, rear spoiler and a tasteful blue and grey interior. They were a commemorative series to celebrate the Viper's 1998 LeMans win. The factory-backed French Oreca team took two Vipers to the most famous endurance race in the world and took 1st and 2nd place. The winning car was driven by World Champion Justin Bell and teammates David Donohue and Luca Drudi. Two other Vipers from the UK-based Chamberlain team ran the race and both finished the gruelling 24 hour course, coming in 5th and 7th. The Vipers also proved to be unstoppable in the '98 GT2 season, with Oreca

1998 Neon R/T. The famous R/T badge appeared on a Neon for the first time in 1998 when a 2-door coupé version went on sale using the 150bhp DOHC engine, and other features taken from the ACR package including quick-ratio steering, sport-tuned suspension, a quick-ratio five-speed manual transmission, four-wheel disc brakes, and an unlimited speed engine controller. Bold Viper stripes and unique 14x6in cast aluminum wheels distinguished the R/T exterior from its siblings. Inside, the R/T boasted a leather steering wheel and shift knob plus unique seat material. It was a popular choice and became particularly sought after by modifiers or tuners who were getting bored with Japanese imports. A host of aftermarket body kits and performance and suspension upgrades soon appeared on the scene.

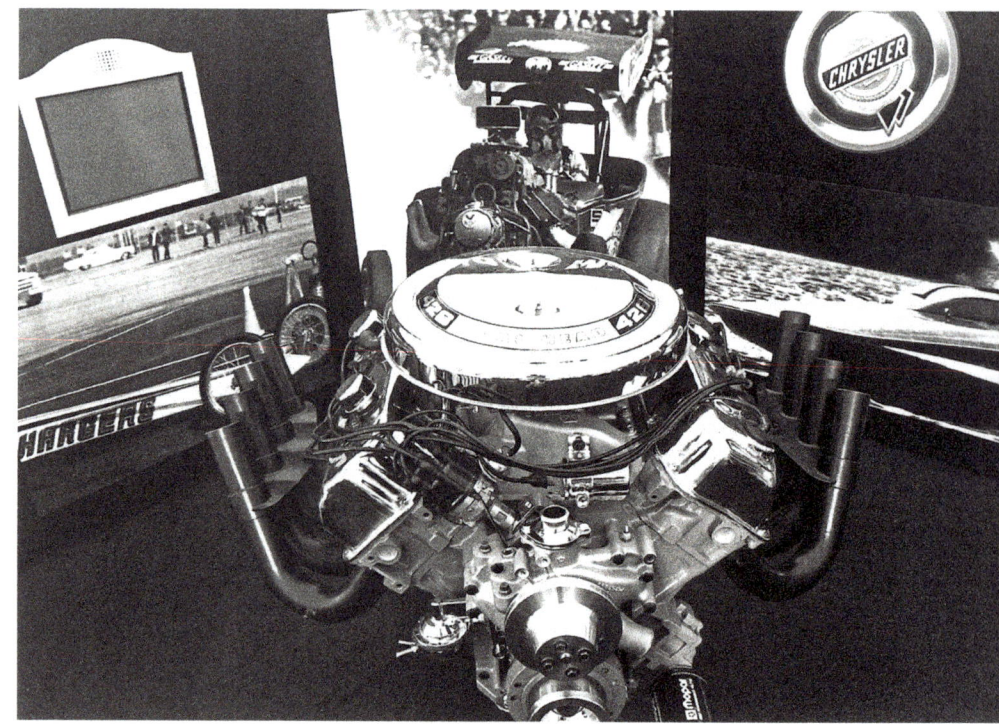

The famed 426in^3 Race Hemi was reintroduced in 1996 as a Crate Hemi. Available only to racers, it was not fitted to any particular car but was sold, as the name suggests, in its packing crate, with most ancillaries attached. The latest Chrysler concept car, the 300 Hemi C convertible, is rumored to have a 426 fitted. The engine shown is an original 426in^3 race Hemi from the late 1960s.

1999 was a very exciting and successful year for Dodge. Yet again, the Oreca team walked away with the FIA GT2 championship and Dodge Vipers (sold as the Chrysler Viper in Europe) took the first six places in the Le Mans 24 hour race. This is Karl Wendliger in the no 92 Viper that Dodge successfully entered in the American Le Mans Series.

The inside of this American Le Mans series Viper GTS-R shows the pure functionality of the race cars. A single Recaro seat with full harness keeps the driver comfortable. A full roll cage, competition wheel and gear shift, and a full set of gauges make up the bare-bones interior of these high-performance vehicles.

taking the championship title for Dodge for the second year in a row. For other types of motorsport, Dodge announced that they were making a 'Crate Hemi' available for racers. As the name suggested, the engine was not fitted into any car but bought, complete with ancillaries, ready to be fitted in to the buyers' vehicle of choice.

If there was doubt as to whether Dodge would continue to make performance cars, its 1998 Charger R/T concept car quashed any doubts. The Supercharged Charger could trace its heritage from the original Charger of 1966. The long nose and short rear-end, the hint of coke-bottle sides and a powerful 4.7-liter V8 engine all add up to a car that blended the best of old and new muscle car styling and performance. At the time, Dodge was teasingly vague as to the future of the Charger R/T but the name, if not this particular

With the Viper's performance in no doubt, people have used the car for some unusual feats. Among them is 36-year-old British man Steve Cunningham who attempted to smash the accompanied World Blind Land Speed Record. Steve is pictured here during his attempt on the runway of RAF Bruntingthorpe in Leicestershire, England.

With his passenger and 'eyes', Peter Colmer Gwynne, Steve smashed the previous blind record of 135.2mph with a run of 147.56 in this 1998 production model GTS, despite atrocious weather conditions. Here Steve (right), along with his guide dog Hughie, celebrates the new world record with the rest of the crew.

Without doubt the most bizarre record attempt must be British journalist Mark Walton's assault on the World Caravan Towing Speed Record. Originally set in Australia in 1991, the world record stood at 126.76mph in a Ford Falcon. Mark used a 1998 production GTS fitted with a specially-made tow bar and a fully-fitted standard Abbey caravan. He set a new record of 127.8mph at RAF Alconbury in Cambridgeshire, England.

Two cars that show just how little difference thirty years can make. Bobby Isaac's championship-winning 1969 Daytona sits in front of a Team Oreca championship-winning 1999 Viper GTS-R. Both cars have the typical low aerodynamic bodies, long nose and short deck of a thoroughbred race car. Both have race-bred engines by Dodge.

Dodge success was not kept exclusively for the Viper in 1999. At the drag strip, Dodge Motorsport Division helped to make world champions. Sheldon Gecker took his Dodge Daytona to victory in the NHRA/Federal-Mogul Super Gas championship, and Frank Manzo won his third consecutive Funny Car title in a Kendall Racing/Team Mopar Avenger. This is Raybestos/Team Mopar's Pro Stock Avenger.

concept, was set to make a glorious return.

Dodge's rekindled interest in muscle cars and motor sports did not appear to be dwindling as they raced towards the new millennium – quite the opposite, in fact. In 1999, Dodge again won LeMans when Vipers staggeringly took the first six places in their class, and once again, Team Oreca won the GT2 championship. Having never left the drag strip, Dodge remained a world-class competitor. Dodge Avenger

driver Laurie Cannister won the Super Eliminator at the IHRA Mopar Finals in August '99, and the Team Mopar top fuel and funny car Dodges were still competing to build on their past successes within the NHRA and World of Outlaws series, winning the LeMans 24 hour for the third consecutive year. A limited amount of lightweight Vipers were built called Viper ACR, and later in the year a Viper ACR Plus. They were street legal cars that were ready to race at the track.

Viper GTS show car. Hot on the heals of the Viper RT/10 open roadster came another show car, this time a hardtop coupé. More than just a design study, rumors of a full production model were rife. When this car hit the auto show circuit in January 1993, public response was overwhelmingly favorable, with customers queuing to place an order. This is the GTS show car at the entrance to the Chrysler test track in Detroit.

2007 Charger Daytona R/T. The first in a series of limited edition cars, the Charger Daytona harked back to the glory days of Mopar muscle, even down to the paint with colors like 'Top Banana', 'Tor Red' and 'GoManGo!.'

For the beginning of a new century, Dodge released an exciting range of cars, almost all of which had a performance version. The new 2000 Neon had an all-new body that used the latest incarnation of Chrysler's 'cab-forward' styling, and an improved 2.0-liter, 16-valve engine. More importantly, the R/T name that first appeared on a performance version of the car in 1998 returned on the next generation of Neon.

The new millennium got off to a great start for Dodge. On 11 January 2000, it rolled out the new Intrepid R/T race car at the North American International Auto Show in Detroit, ahead of its inaugural race at the 2001 Daytona 500. The Viper scored one of its most welcome wins at the beginning of 2000 when it beat its arch-rival, the Chevrolet Corvette, taking the checkered flag at the Daytona 24 hour race outright – the first time that a GTS-class car had won the event for more than 20 years. Following that, the GTS then came in 1-2-3 at the 12-hour race at Sebring in March, once again trouncing the factory-backed Vette. In Europe, the Viper continued to race as a Chrysler, and won the 2000 LeMans GTS Class for the third year in a row.

Production vehicles saw a major overhaul with a development of the cab-forward ethos. One of the first cars designed with the aid of Virtual Reality computers, the second generation Neon took just 28 months to develop. The 2-door coupé had gone, along with the DOHC engine, leaving only a 4-door sedan with a SOHC 4-cylinder Magnum engine. It looked heavier and less nimble, more mature somehow, and carried the new family-look front grille. The performance model was again the R/T, but some motoring journalists criticized the use of the prestigious 'R/T' badge on a car that wasn't that fast or furious.

One Neon that was very quick was the SRT concept, which debuted at the Los Angeles Auto Show on 6 January 2000 alongside the Viper GTSR concept. The Neon SRT was the most powerful Neon thus far. With a supercharged, 2.0-liter, 16-valve engine that generated 208hp, the SRT showed the potential Neon had in its latest guise. The Stratus, Avenger and Intrepid received a slight facelift until 2001, when they got a complete makeover. The Mitsubishi-built Avenger became the Stratus coupé for 2001, selling beside the Chrysler-built 4-door Stratus sedan. Available as an R/T, the Stratus coupé was the performance pick of the bunch, which featured an all-new (for the Stratus) 3.0-liter V6 option. More refined and with better build-quality and power, they were well received. The following year saw the Stratus sedans receiving the revised front ends along with an R/T option for the Chrysler-based 4-doors.

On 14 October 1999, it was announced that after a break of 18 long years, Dodge would be returning to NASCAR stockcar racing for the 2001 Winston Cup Series. The first race, at the prestigious Daytona 500, proved a promising start when Dodge Intrepids won the first three positions at the start line, but on the day, success eluded them. Dodge fielded ten cars from as many teams. Sterling Marlin (#40) led countless laps and

The 2000 Stratus ES steps up a size from the Neon, to blend performance with the practicality of an intermediate-sized car. Powered by a 168bhp V6, the ES had an AutoStick transaxle, which allows the driver to choose between auto or manual shift, a new performance suspension and unique tires on cast-aluminum wheels. Dodge brand's core philosophy was bold, powerful and capable. The Stratus certainly covered that.

Along with the Stratus, the Avenger ES carried the Dodge performance ideals to buyers of mid-size cars in a very sporty looking package. Only available as a coupé, it came with a 24-valve, single overhead cam SMPI 152.3in³ V6 as standard. An R/T version was released early in the new millennium to join the Intrepid and Neon R/Ts.

2001 NASCAR Intrepid. On 14 October 1999, Dodge Vice President Jim Julow announced the long-awaited news that the division was finally ready to go back into stock car racing. This historic move back to the NASCAR/Winston Cup series finally gave Dodge performance fans a team to cheer. This is an artist's impression of the Intrepid-based stock car Dodge intended to use ...

finished in 7th position. Ward Burton went out after getting involved in the 18-car crash that took the life of racing legend Dale Earnhardt Snr, and Bill Elliot, who started in pole position, finished in 5th place overall. Success came close on many occasions after that first race but Dodge would have to wait until 19 August to see Sterling Marlin take the checkered flag at Michigan International Speedway for its first NASCAR Winston Cup win. When Dodge returned to Florida for the 2002 series Daytona 500, it won.

... and this is what it looked like in the flesh. Not since the glory days of the late sixties and early seventies had Mopar backed a stock car program. It had intended to run at least two teams for the inaugural race at the Daytona 500, held on 24 February 2001. On the day, it had ten cars from as many teams, but success eluded them. When the Intrepid returned to Daytona in 2002 it took the checkered flag.

This is Kyle Petty in May 2000, putting the Dodge Intrepid R/T test car through its paces at Homestead Miami Speedway ...

2001 Neon R/T. With the demise of the 2-door coupé at the end of 1999, the 4-door R/T version of the Mk2 Neon became the performance compact car. The R/T and the lightweight ACR shared the same 4-cylinder, 16-valve SOHC, 2.0-liter Magnum engine. This motor generated 150hp at 5700rpm, and 136lb-ft at 4800rpm. In order to get the same horsepower out of the R/T's SOHC engine that the former DOHC generated, the ports were opened up and a new aluminum long-port intake manifold and welded tubular steel header were fitted. The camshaft was also revised for longer duration and higher lift. The R/T sat on larger than standard 16in alloy wheels and tires to help handling. Estimated performance was a respectable 0-60mph in 7.7 seconds and a top speed of 129mph. Only available with a 5-speed manual gearbox, this offered an impressive 28mpg.

For 2002, the Neon went unchanged, but for the first time the Stratus could be had with a manual 5-speed gearbox mated to a V6, and the sedan now had an R/T version. In May of that year, the last Viper coupé was made. This was celebrated by making the last 360 units as a special limited edition, called the GTS Final Edition. It came with unique paintwork, red-stitched, black leather steering wheel and shift knob, and a sequentially numbered dash plaque (e.g. No. 1 of 360) recognizing each individual car from the series. It could be purchased with the optional ACR performance package. The end of the coupé was to make way for the most powerful Dodge to date, the new Viper SRT10 roadster.

Looking very much like the Viper GTSR concept from the previous year, the new production Viper was officially launched as a 2003 model. The SRT10 (Street and Racing Technology 10-cylinder) was the next chapter in Viper history and set the standard for American

2001 Neon ACR. As with the first incarnation of the Neon ACR, the 2001 version was aimed at grass-roots racers. Similar to the R/T front fascia, the Neon ACR package included a lower air dam and grille insert. However, unlike the R/T, it did not include fog lamps. The ACR also featured the dual exhaust of the R/T, along with the suspension, but omitted the side skirts to save weight. The standard wheels become the 15in WJA 'Impulse' wheels, optional on the LE/LX & SE/ES models. Unlike the first generation of ACR Neons, which sold in Canada and the USA, the Mk2 was not available outside America.

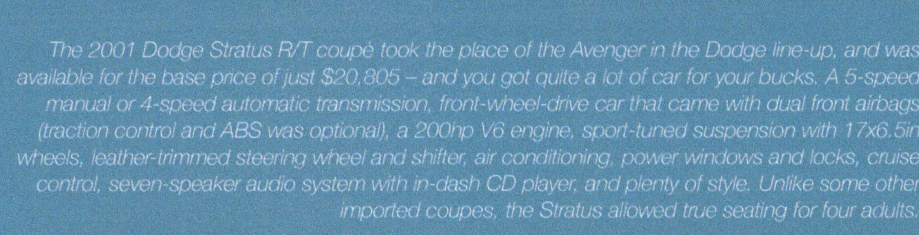

The 2001 Dodge Stratus R/T coupé took the place of the Avenger in the Dodge line-up, and was available for the base price of just $20,805 – and you got quite a lot of car for your bucks. A 5-speed manual or 4-speed automatic transmission, front-wheel-drive car that came with dual front airbags (traction control and ABS was optional), a 200hp V6 engine, sport-tuned suspension with 17x6.5in wheels, leather-trimmed steering wheel and shifter, air conditioning, power windows and locks, cruise control, seven-speaker audio system with in-dash CD player, and plenty of style. Unlike some other imported coupes, the Stratus allowed true seating for four adults.

sports cars throughout the industry. This time Dodge wanted to build a true convertible version of the original Dodge Viper RT/10 roadster, but at the same time, refine the original caricature without losing its outrageous design. With over one hundred improvements, including a more powerful engine and lighter, more streamlined body, it stayed true to the goals of the first Vipers: a front-engined, two-seat, rear-wheel-drive sports car. With a new bored and stroked aluminum engine block that increased the Viper's displacement from 488 to 505in^3 and pushed its V10 power output to 500 horsepower and 525lb-ft of torque, Viper had no equal on the road.

To pick up the racing baton, a coupé version of the new SRT10 was unleashed at the same time as the convertible, called simply, the competition coupé. Built in very limited numbers (less than 30) and only available to registered racers, the single-seat competition coupé came track-ready, and although largely based on the SRT10 soft top, the competition coupé developed 20 more horsepower (520bhp) and 15 more lb-ft of torque (540lb-ft) than the street-going version. Interestingly, the

2002 Viper Final Edition. In May 2002, the last Viper GTS coupé rolled down the assembly line followed by the craftsmen who built it. The last 360s built were designated GTS Final Edition models and came with unique paintwork, a red-stitched interior, black leather steering wheel and shift knob, and a sequentially numbered dash plaque.

2002 Viper shoot out. The challenge pitted the all-new Dodge Viper against an F-16 jet in a side-by-side, standing-start, half-mile drag race on parallel air base runways, accelerating to the speed at which the jet became airborne – approximately 150mph. The Dodge Viper covered the course in around 15 seconds, beating the F-16 and winning the competition.

2003 Viper SRT10 roadster. Originally unveiled at the 2001 North American International Auto Show as the RT/10, it offered a first look at the third chapter in the Dodge Viper history. It was a true convertible with a more powerful V10 engine (500hp, 500 lb-ft of torque and 505in^3 displacement), and a new design inspired by the GTSR concept. It went on sale in fall of 2002 as a 2003 model. Known internally by the code VGX, the RT/10 was renamed the Dodge Viper SRT10 in January 2002. The SRT10 roadster was fitted with an 8.3-liter V10 engine, heavy-duty six-speed manual transmission, and other high-performance treatments befitting an SRT vehicle. A true convertible, the Viper SRT10 roadster offered a bi-fold clamshell top. The roof featured a rigid cloth-covered front panel, glass rear window, and a single center latch on the windshield header.

competition coupé and the new convertible had proved their performance capabilities long before they were released to the public.

Over the weekend of 23 and 24 March 2002, the oddest but most spectacular drag race occurred in Glendale, Arizona. Filmed for the *Ripley's Believe It Or Not* TV programme, USAF F-16 Vipers were pitted against a pre-production SRT10 convertible and a prototype competition coupé, to find out who had the

2003 Viper competition coupé (plus interior and engine). Based very much on the GTSR concept, the competition coupé was a closed-cockpit competition model. With concept car bodywork, full racing cage and other safety features, this was an affordable, limited production race car for competition-oriented owners. The coupé developed 20 more horsepower (520 bhp) and 15 more lb-ft of torque (540lb-ft) than the street-going convertible. Power was enhanced via a performance camshaft and tuned exhaust. Production was limited to 25-30 race cars, with plans for expansion on demand, but they were only available to registered racing licence holders who were participants in the SCCA Speedvision World Challenge, Grand American Grand-Am Cup Class and the Skip Thomas Viper Racing League.

fastest Viper. The programme did an amazing job of convincing the General in charge of Luke Airforce Base in Glendale, Arizona and the guys at Chrysler's proving grounds, also in Arizona, to put the race on within the Luke Air Show. Brigadier General Sargeant supplied not one but two of the $30,000,000 F-16s, nicknamed Vipers, for the showdown to see who was fastest across a ½ mile track.

The plan was to run two drag races, one with the SRT10 pitted against one of the F-16s that would not use its afterburner, and the second race between the competition coupé and the other F-16 that *would* use its afterburner. Drop flags and cameras were placed at the ¼ and ½-mile point. Everything was set.

In front of a 140,000 strong crowd, the first two racers prepared. As the F-16 warmed up, the driver of the SRT10, Herb Helbig, readied the Viper's tires with a quick burnout, then they lined up and the start flag was dropped.

The Viper rocketed forward while the F-16 jet lumbered off the line. At the ¼-mile mark, it was the Dodge's flag that dropped first, and by the final ½-mile the SRT10 was still out in the lead. 1-0 to Dodge. Ready for round two!

In its most basic form, an afterburner is the equivalent of a 'nitros' kit on a car; it uses leftover fuel in the burnt gases to increase thrust enormously. This is what the competition coupé would be up against. Piloted once again by Herb, the Viper warmed up its racing tires and both vehicles lined up. As the flag dropped, both engines roared and the Viper hurtled forward, again taking the lead. A 30ft flame shot from the back of the jet fighter as it rolled forward. Eleven seconds later, it was the Dodge that dropped their flag first at the ¼-mile point but the F-16 was catching up fast. At the ½-mile flag it was neck-and-neck for a photo finish that showed they were perfectly aligned. A split second later the F-16 rotated and climbed vertically into the clear Arizona sky with the pilot calling over the radio "Hey Herbie, TRY THIS!" So the result was Dodge wins!

WORLDLY WISE

Along with other automotive manufacturers, Chrysler was intent on building more 'world cars', vehicles that could be recognized and sold, with little modification, around the globe. The Neon, along with Chrysler's PT Cruiser and Dodge's minivans, were Chrysler's main armament in this attack. With its continuing success in Europe and other parts of the world, Chrysler drove home the attack with the Crossfire, and later with the C-300 and Dodge Magnum. Building on this, Dodge released a string of concept cars in 2003 and 2004. Some of these concepts,

like the Avenger and rear-wheel-drive, Hemi-powered Magnum SRT8 tourer and SRT4, were very close to what Dodge expected production vehicles to look like. Others were used as a bold statement of where Dodge was and where it wanted to go.

The 4-wheeled Tomahawk motorcycle was the pinnacle of this. An outlandish, ridiculous and stunning piece of automotive art, at its official launch at the 2003 North American International Auto Show, Trevor Creed, Senior VP – Design, stated, "This is a bold faced slap against mediocrity, Tomahawk is a scintillating example of what creative minds can do when given the opportunity to run free".

The Stratus coupes carried a revised front-end and most standard Dodge cars made in 2003 were available as either an R/T or a sporty SXT model, with the larger cars using either 2.4-liter or 3.5-liter V6s.

Even the humble Neon now had the option of a 2.0-liter Magnum engine that was still good for 150hp. But it still wasn't quite enough for the Dodge boys, and 2003 saw the launch of the Neon-based SRT4.

Production of the SRT4 started in the spring of 2003 at the Belvidere (Illinois) Assembly Plant, alongside standard Neons, but this was no standard issue car. Based on the Neon SRT concept vehicle first introduced at the turn of the century and the later SRT4 concept, the production Dodge SRT4 combined performance

It had been more than 30 years since Dodge ruled the streets with Hemi power and rear-wheel-drive performance, but in spring of 2004 production began on the new rear-wheel-drive Magnum, selling as a 2005 model. The base Magnum came with a potent 2.7-liter V6 engine, or a 3.5-liter version in the SXT, but the R/T version was about to make history. The Magnum RT – along with its Chrysler 300 sister – were the first modern, high-volume production vehicles in North America to feature fully functioning cylinder deactivation as standard equipment with the 5.7-liter Hemi engine. The Multi-Displacement System (MDS) seamlessly alternates between smooth, high fuel economy 4-cylinder mode when less power is needed and V8 mode when more power from the 5.7-liter Hemi engine is in demand. This optimizes fuel economy when V8 power is not needed, without sacrificing vehicle performance. In its first year of production, 43 per cent of buyers went for the Hemi V8 option.

2003 SRT4. The new Neon-based SRT4 offered superior drivability from a compact production car that was almost unheard of in its price range. Agile handling capability was made possible by 17in aluminum performance wheels, 50 series tires, specially tuned strut and spring assemblies (front and rear), sway bars (front and rear), updated knuckles and a unique K-member. Match all that to a 2.4-liter turbo-boosted 205hp engine, and the end result is a vehicle that can accelerate from 0-60mph in 5.9 seconds straight out of the factory, making it the quickest car in the Dodge line-up, second only to the Dodge Viper SRT10. Power like that also made it the quickest production car available in the United States priced under $20,000! If that was not enough, upgrade kits from the Mopar division could push horsepower past the 300 mark. Interesting to note that the name Neon was never associated with the SRT4, as Chrysler wanted to distance the new hot car from the sometimes maligned standard fare.

The Dodge Charger – one of the biggest names from the muscle car era – powered its way back to streets and racetracks across America, paying homage to the muscle cars of the '60s, and adding 21st century performance and functionality. In standard form, it came with the 250 horsepower, 3.5-liter High-Output V6 engine shared with the Magnum, or the legendary 340 horsepower, 5.7-liter Hemi V8 engine. Dodge designers sculpted a vehicle that celebrates all that is good about American cars, in a thoroughly modern way. The profile of the Dodge Charger's roofline and the sloping fastback style suggest a sense of speed. It has a long character line that defines the front corners, runs back to the rear door, and makes way for a huge rear fender that lets you know this car is rear-wheel-drive. With the longest wheelbase in its class, the Dodge Charger offers a spacious interior, with the seating position more than two inches higher than the previous generation Dodge sedan.

MICHIGAN INTERNATIONAL SPEEDWAY .

with features inspired entirely by the street-racing scene. The result was a vehicle that could accelerate from 0-60mph in 5.9 seconds straight out of the factory, making it the quickest car in the Dodge lineup, second only to the Dodge Viper SRT10. Power like this also made it the quickest production car available in the United States priced under $20,000! The power was coming from a 2.4-liter, DOHC, turbo-boosted, 205hp, in-line 4-cylinder engine, which delivered 220lb-ft of torque available from 2000 to 4800rpm, and could top 152mph. If that was not enough, upgrade kits from the Mopar division could push

horsepower past the 300 mark. Other production cars went very much unchanged, except the Stratus sedan, which received a makeover to match the Stratus coupé.

With its introduction of the minivan or MPV (multi-purpose vehicle) back in the early eighties, Chrysler sealed the fate of the station wagon, and twenty-something years later it was Chrysler that was reinventing the wheel with the introduction of a whole new generation of classic American station wagons. It was in May 2004 that the first Dodge production car in over 33 years to be powered by a Hemi engine went on sale – the Magnum.

The Magnum arrived as a 2005 model, and was based on the new rear-wheel drive LX platform. The cab-forward look that had been so successful for Chrysler through the late nineties and into the new millennium was coming to an end, and was being replaced by a more traditional American style that favored rear-wheel drive, a long nose, short deck and a high belt line, reminiscent of Virgil Exner's designs from the fifties. The Magnum and its Chrysler 300C cousin were typical of this new design emphasis. Oddly, perhaps, Chrysler decided not to offer the 300C Tourer as a companion to the 300C sedan in the American market. The station wagon-bodied tourer was given to the Dodge Magnum. Available in three models, the introductory SE, the SXT and sporty R/T, the base models came with a potent 3.5-liter V6, but the R/T ... well, that had the all-new Hemi.

First seen in the Chrysler 300 Hemi C concept car, the new Hemi boasted 5.7-liters of adrenalin-pumping power that produced 340hp. The new Hemi was based on the legendary engine that powered Dodge's muscle cars of the 1960s, but re-engineered and reborn as a modern, high-performance, fuel-efficient power plant known as the 'all-new 5.7-liter Hemi V8'. Using that 340 horsepower and 390lb-ft of torque, the Dodge Magnum RT could go from zero to 60mph in just 6.3 seconds. It also took the record for being the first modern production vehicle in North America to feature cylinder deactivation. The Multi-Displacement System (MDS) seamlessly turns off the fuel consumption in four cylinders of the engine when V8 power is not needed, giving a combination of performance and fuel economy. All this power is sent back to the rear wheels through an independent five-bar rear-drive layout.

2005 saw the long awaited

The standard suspension offered on the 2006 Dodge Charger R/T model includes massive 18in touring tires and wheels, and specially tuned dampers for ride and handling, with a performance exhaust. A Road/Track Performance Group, which is tuned specifically for firm steering and handling, provides 18in Michelin MXM4 all-season performance tires, 9-land performance steering gear and Nivomat self-leveling shock absorbers. A specially-tuned performance exhaust and induction system, which produces an additional 10 horsepower from the Hemi V8 engine, is also included with the R/T package.

return of another much-loved nameplate, the Charger. Released as a 2006 model, the new Charger was again based on the LX platform and featured smooth fastback styling along with four-door practicality. Initially available in SE and SXT models and fitted with a base 3.5-liter V6, it wasn't long before Dodge started releasing more performance versions of this car. Maximizing the legendary names of the classic muscle car era, the Charger R/T and Daytona R/T were released in

familiar tones: 'GoManGo!' 'Top Banana' and 'Tor Red' were issued in limited numbers. These cars all had the new, 5.7-liter Hemi as fitted to the Magnum, Chrysler 300C and some Jeep models, with the Daytona receiving a 350bhp version.

To celebrate the release of the Charger, Dodge announced a new Charger race car for the 2005 NASCAR Nextel Cup series, replacing the Intrepid. Unfortunately, the new car did not live up to expectations and throughout the 2005 series,

The 2006 Dodge Charger and Magnum police vehicles began production in September 2005, and were armed with modern muscle and superior rear-wheel-drive performance. They were fitted with the latest advanced systems including all-speed traction control system (TCS), electronic stability program (ESP) with brake assist and four-wheel anti-lock disc brake system (ABS), and a host of extra equipment to make crime prevention easier. The powerful 5.7-liter Hemi engine and rear-wheel-drive setup of the Magnum and Charger made them ideal candidates for the Police Vehicle Evaluation Program, which included a series of grueling on-road tests assessing acceleration, top speed, braking, and vehicle dynamics. Both the Charger and Magnum excelled in these challenges.

Jeremy Mayfield, at the wheel of his No 19 Dodge Dealers/UAW Dodge Charger, attending a press conference to debut the newly designed Dodge Charger race car during NASCAR Nextel Cup testing on 11 January 2005, at the Daytona International Speedway in Daytona Beach, Florida. Unfortunately, the new Charger failed to live up to expectations on the track.

Dodge Motorsports did have some success in 2005 when Gary Scelzi piloted the Mopar/Oakley Dodge Stratus R/T to the National Hot Rod Association's (NHRA) POWERade Funny Car title. Scelzi joins Kenny Bernstein as only the second driver to win titles in NHRA's Funny Car and Top Fuel classes.

2005 competition coupé & SRT10 roadster. Paying homage to the 1996 GTS, the SRT10 coupé was a contemporary take on that design. Although similar in looks to the roadster, the only bodywork that the SRT10 coupé shares with the roadster is the front fascia and fenders, bonnet and doors. Besides the new canopy and decklid, the new Dodge Viper SRT10 coupé has a special windshield surround, door side glass, rear fascia, quarter panels and tail lamps. This was the street version of the 2003 competition coupé that was as comfortable on the road as it was on the track. Many Viper owners regularly race their cars, and with an engine that offers 500hp and a 0 to 100mph time of just 12 seconds, why not? The Dodge Viper SRT10 coupé and roadster are built at the Conner Avenue Assembly Plant in Detroit, Michigan.

Dodge teams considered going back to their now tried and tested Intrepid. Talk of a more aerodynamic nose for the Charger was bandied around but not agreed on by NASCAR officials.

Dodge Motorsports did have some success in 2005, however, when Gary Scelzi piloted the Mopar/Oakley Dodge Stratus R/T to the National Hot Rod Association's (NHRA) POWERade Funny Car title, while Ted Musgrave drove the no 1 Ultra Motorsports Mopar Dodge Ram to the National Association for Stock Car Auto Racing (NASCAR) Craftsman Truck Series championship.

Another important release for Dodge this year happened on 1 March at the Geneva Motor Show in Switzerland, when it unveiled the latest Viper – the SRT10 coupé. Once again, sold as a 2006 model, the all-American sports car boasted an aluminum block 8.3-liter V10 engine that offered the impressive numbers of 500/500/500. Initially released in Viper blue with twin white racing stripes, the coupé had 500 horsepower, 525lb-ft of torque and 505in^3 of displacement. Transferring all of this power to the rear wheels is a heavy-duty six-speed manual transmission, which accelerates the car to 100mph in 12.5 seconds. By far the better looking of the

2006 6.1-liter Hemi. This is what all the fuss was about. Not happy with the 5.7-liter version of the new Hemi engine, Chrysler released an even more powerful 6.1-liter version, boosting horsepower to 425. It still utilized Chrysler's MDS system to deactivate four of the eight cylinders when not required in heavy traffic, then supplied neck-wrenching power from all eight when the accelerator was pushed hard.

2006 Charger SRT8. With its launch in late 2006 for the 2007 model year, the SRT8 became the fastest sedan in the Dodge family. The Hemi engine was boosted to 425hp from its 6.1-liter capacity, enabling the SRT8 to accelerate from 0 to 60mph in under 5.5 seconds, and up to 100mph less than 10 seconds later.

2005 Neon SXT. This was the last year for the Neon. The R/T had been dropped so, except for the SRT4, the SXT became the only performance model. Standard SXT features included body-color door handles and moldings, power door locks, power front windows, air conditioning, AM/FM stereo with CD player and six speakers, remote keyless entry, a power trunk lid release, and 15in all-season touring tires with aluminum wheels. An optional SRT sport appearance package was available on the SXT which included unique 15in aluminum wheels, an SRT4-type power bulge hood, fog lamps, a unique color center stack, and automatic shifter bezel with the automatic transaxle and twin exhaust pipes.

pair, the coupé shares only its front clip and doors with the roadster, with all other bodywork unique to the hardtop.

The release of all these new vehicles meant that Neon's time was almost up. In its final year, the R/T was dropped, but the SXT received a beefed up package including the hood from the current SRT4. On 22 September 2005, the 2,388,135th and very last Neon – a normal, unspectacular white 4-door – rolled off the production line at the Belvidere Assembly Plant in Illinois as a 2006 model. As the last car rolled down the assembly line, plant mechanics followed close behind, reorganizing the line for the next build, Dodge's new compact – the Caliber.

Based very much on the Caliber show car of 2005, this chunky compact is based on a platform developed with Mitsubishi, which it shares with the second

2006 Charger GT. If standard trim wasn't enough, the GT sport package offered an array of bolt-on extras, including a hexagon grille insert, cat-back exhaust system ending in dual chrome tips, rear facia air diffuser, and special 17in 5-spoke chrome wheels.

2006 Caliber SRT4. Caliber, along with the Nitro SUV, was Dodge's main armament in its attack on European markets. In America, the Caliber was released in SE, SXT, R/T and SRT4 models. Just one month after the Caliber's launch, Chrysler's Performance Vehicle Operations (PVO) team released the twelfth vehicle to carry the SRT badge. The Street and Racing Technology vehicles are built to be at home on both track and normal roads. The Caliber SRT4 takes over from the Neon-based SRT4 as Dodge's 'pocket-rocket'. Performance and handling that supply 0 to 60 times of less than 6 seconds, with fuel economy of 28mpg, is the best of both worlds.

To achieve its high-performance, the SRT4 is fitted with a supercharged aluminum 2.4-liter World Engine, specially machined for increased water and oil flow. Unique cast pistons travel within iron cylinder liners, cooled by oil squirters and affixed to forged connecting rods, offering performance usually attributed to much larger V8 engines. The SRT4 is just one of the Caliber derivatives being sold in Europe and other world markets in left- and right-hand-drive forms, and comes in four exterior colors: Brilliant Black, Sunburst Orange, Bright Silver and Inferno Red.

2007 Charger Daytona R/T. The first Charger Daytona deliveries were made to dealers in August 2005. To celebrate, thirty-three Daytonas, all finished in 'GoManGo!' paintwork, cruised from the Walter P Chrysler museum and down Detroit's famous Woodward Avenue, escorted by Dodge police cars. Other classic colors included 'Top Banana' and 'Tor Red'. The Daytona isn't just a different shade of paint – the Hemi engine received an extra 10hp from its 5.7 liters, boosting bhp to 350. In addition, the Daytona R/T model is distinguishable by a black honeycomb grille, black 'Daytona' and 'Hemi' decals, signature heritage R/T badging, and a black rear decklid spoiler.

2007 Charger Daytona R/T. The first in a series of limited edition cars, the Charger Daytona harked back to the glory days of Mopar muscle. Tastefully executed, the Daytona carried 4-door styling particularly well.

With its launch in late 2006 for the 2007 model year, the SRT8 became the fastest sedan in the Dodge family. The Hemi engine was boosted to 425hp from its 6.1-liter capacity, enabling the SRT8 to accelerate from 0 to 60mph in less than 5.5 seconds and up to 100mph under 10 seconds later. The SuperBee made great use of the nostalgia for its 1970 namesake when released as a limited edition, along with the Daytona. The SuperBee carried familiar markings on its bright Detonator Yellow paintwork, accentuated by the black hood.

generation PT Cruiser and Chrysler Sebring. Styling follows the DaimlerChrysler bosses belief that the day of small sedans has gone, so the hatchback or station wagon is the way to go. Chrysler is hoping that this high, stubby 'cross-over' vehicle can take on the world. Along with the Jeep-type Nitro, the Caliber went on sale in the UK and across Europe in 2006 as Dodge's introduction to those markets and Chrysler's replacement for its Neon. By early 2007, the European Dodge range had been strengthened with the Caliber SRT4, a turbocharged 2.4-liter-powered version that offered 300hp and a 0 to 60 time of less than 6 seconds. The Stratus was in its final year in 2006, and with no 2-door coupé anywhere in the Dodge range, the hope is the resurrection of another classic name from the Seventies will be back with the return of the Challenger, which at present remains a concept car.

In late 2006, Dodge released another limited edition car for the 2007 model year, the Charger SRT8 SuperBee. Described as the first special edition of a 'Charger on steroids' by Chrysler's Street and Racing Technology team, the SRT8 is the most powerful Charger yet, with its 6.1-liter, 425hp Hemi V8, it has the capability to achieve 100mph in less than 17 seconds. This makes it Dodge's quickest sedan. The SuperBee is painted in 'Detonator Yellow' exterior color with black hood and deck-lid face, SuperBee logos on front and rear fenders, and contrasting yellow stitching on the seats, steering wheel and shift knob.

Chrysler is looking at plans to introduce a low-cost vehicle, smaller than the Caliber and Nitro, as soon as 2009, although the difficulty would be where to build it. A performance version would be sure to follow, but for now, admirers of performance vehicles – and Dodge in particular – still have a large choice and the immediate future of muscle cars is looking very good. The new breed of R/T vehicles and special edition SRT cars makes full use of legendary names from days gone by, tapping into the trend for nostalgia but adding a contemporary twist. On 1st July, 2006, Chrysler CEO Tom LaSorda announced that due to overwhelming response from the public, the Challenger concept will go into production for 2008 and at the Paris Mondial de l'Automobile show in September 2006, DaimlerChrysler unveiled their next D-segment car for Europe and America – the muscular Avenger 4-door sedan, which went into production in the Spring of 2007. The Avenger also joined the Charger on the race track in NASCAR's 'Car of Tomorrow' series. As Dodge celebrate 50 years of making performance cars, what better way to celebrate than to enter new markets with a selection of its finest ... but wouldn't it be nice if it offered a D-500 edition, to help celebrate its anniversary? Whichever way you look at it though, it is a great time to 'grab life by the horns!' and GO DODGE.

IT'S A GO!

Challenger

Auburn Hills, Michigan, 1 July 2006 – Chrysler Group President and CEO Tom LaSorda announced that Dodge Challenger will return to production after a nearly 35-year hiatus. The all-new Dodge Challenger will debut as a 2008 model in calendar year 2008. The announcement was made shortly before the Pepsi 400 NASCAR race at Daytona International Speedway in Daytona Beach, Florida.

"We haven't seen this kind of spontaneous, passionate response to a car since we unveiled the Dodge Viper concept in 1989," said LaSorda. "But it's easy to see what people like about the Dodge Challenger. It's bold, powerful and capable. It's a modern take on one of the most iconic muscle cars, and sets a new standard for pure pony car performance."

2008 Challenger. On the 13 February 2007, DaimlerChrysler announced that the all-new 2008 Dodge Challenger will be built at its Brampton Assembly Plant near Toronto, alongside the Chrysler 300, Dodge Charger and Dodge Magnum.

2008 Avenger is an all-new, medium-sized sedan that combines bold, aggressive Dodge styling with innovative interior features, high-levels of safety and reliability, exhilarating performance, and potential fuel efficiency of up to 30mpg. Available in SE, SXT and R/T models, along with an R/T AWD (All Wheel Drive) version, the performance R/Ts come with a 3.5-liter V6 engine that boasts 235 horsepower and 232lb-ft of torque. This all-new mid-size sedan also marks a milestone in the Dodge brand's car renaissance. From Viper to Caliber and every segment in-between, Dodge now offers an extremely competitive and sporty car.

2008 Avenger. Production of the 2008 Dodge Avenger began in the fourth quarter of 2006, at the refurbished Sterling Heights Assembly Plant in Michigan, alongside the Chrysler Sebring and Sebring Convertible. Avenger's 173 horsepower, 2.4-liter four-cylinder World Engine is built in the state-of-the art Global Engine Manufacturing Alliance (GEMA) plant in Dundee, Michigan. The 2.7-liter, V6 engine and the 3.5-liter, V6 engine are built at the Kenosha (Wisconsin) Engine Plant.

The Dodge Avenger race car joined the Dodge Charger in NASCAR NEXTEL Cup competition on the 25 March 2007, when it made its racing debut in the Food City 500 at Bristol Motor Speedway, the first NASCAR Car of Tomorrow (COT) race. The COT program is a collaborative effort by the sanctioning body, manufacturers, teams and industry suppliers to develop a safer, less expensive race car using a more common design. Mixed feelings about the new design of race car were aired after the race. Dodge's highest place was 13th.

The 1991 Neon, with its happy-faced headlights and sub-compact, cab-forward design, was created to appeal to a younger market. At its inception and through development to the production vehicle of 1994, many other styles were proposed, including a roadster version and a race car. Some of these never got past the drawing board stage, whilst others were actually built.

It would be hard to look at Dodge performance cars and not mention the concept cars or dream cars. The vehicles built to test technological advancement and public reaction to styling cues. All modern production vehicles develop from these concept cars, evolving into working prototypes, then pre-production models and onto the finished article we purchase. The first idea car of note was the Buick 'Y' job of 1938, penned by the legendary GM design chief, Harley Earl. From then on, the automotive world moved quickly to bring out fresher, faster and more ultra-modern vehicles in a huge game of one-upmanship

with their competitors. Today, DaimlerChrysler differs from many manufacturers with regard to its concept cars. Whereas most automakers never get their designs further than one-off 'idea-cars', DaimlerChrysler led the world in exhibiting exciting concepts and then putting them into production almost unchanged. Along the way, there have been some quite stunning and beautiful creations ... alongside more ridiculous ventures.

1954 FIREARROW SPORT COUPE

In 1954, Dodge released its first significant concept cars with a series of Firearrow dream cars, all based on the Dodge production vehicles of that year. With its low hood and sloping rear deck, the Firearrow was a beautiful blend of typical American roadster styling and European sports car design, ensuring a long, low and wide 2-seater sports car. It was this design that inspired the low-production Dual-Ghia sports car from 1956. The roadster featured an unframed one-piece windshield, bumperless fuselage and Italian wood-rimmed steering wheel. As with most of Chrysler's concept cars of the period, the sport coupé was hand-built by Ghia of Turin, Italy and was a development of the roadster, with an added coupé hardtop and revised concave grille and bumpers. Finished in metallic opal blue, it was a beautiful car, and fast. With its specially modified new 241.3in³ Red Ram Hemi V8 engine, mated to a Powerflite automatic gearbox, this car was used to set a new woman's speed record when Miss Betty Skelton achieved 143.44mph at Chrysler's proving grounds.

1954 – FireArrow Sport Coupe Dodge's first idea car, the Firearrow was a sublime mix of typical American roadster styling and European sports car ideas. There were four cars with the nameplate; the first two were 2-seater convertibles, the third a handsome hardtop sport coupé (pictured) and the last a 4-seater convertible. All built by Ghia of Turin and powered by Dodge's Hemi V8, the coupé achieved a top speed of 143.44mph when it was driven by a Miss Betty Skelton at Chrysler's proving grounds.

The 1961 Dodge FliteWing experimental car was very much Lancer-based. Built in Italy by Ghia, it was a running vehicle that had easy access and egress for the occupants as its main theme. Two power-assisted, flip-up windows rose when the door handle was touched and remained open until the door was shut, whereupon the windows would automatically close. Inside the car four bucket seats gave a cockpit-like feel, and driver information was emphasized with a modern-looking instrument panel that gave updates on fuel, engine temperature, amperage and oil pressure, along with turn signals, full beam indicator and parking brake light.

THE 1961 FLITEWING

This was also built by Ghia of Turin, and was based very much on the Lancer. It was a running vehicle built to examine easier ways of entering and exiting cars. The car featured hydraulically operated flip-up side windows, which rose when the door opened and remained in an upright position until the door closed. This design eliminated the center C-pillar and cleverly, when the door was closed, allowed the windows to still be operated in a conventional manor.

THE 1964 CHARGER

The 1964 Charger show car was Dodge division's interpretation of a performance car of the near future. In the hope of attracting more sales, Dodge made no effort to hide its use of '64 Polara sheet metal and chassis. The Charger featured a large hood scoop, competition-height windshield, dash-mounted rev counter and integral roll-bar. Dual exhausts exited the car from pipes that finished in chrome rectangles, which appeared through the panel behind the doors. And being a Chrysler Corporation car, this was no empty model. It was fully operational, and what else could Dodge use for power in a performance concept but the mighty 426 Hemi competition engine?

The 1964 Charger show car was Dodge Division's interpretation of a performance car of the near future. In the hope of attracting more sales, Dodge made no effort to hide its use of '64 Polara sheet metal and chassis. The Charger featured a large hood scoop, competition-height windshield, dash-mounted rev counter and integral roll bar. Dual exhausts exited the car from pipes that finished in chrome rectangles, which came through the panel behind the doors. And being a Chrysler Corporation car, this was no empty model – it was fully working, and what could Dodge use for power in a performance concept car except the mighty 426 Hemi competition engine?

THE 1965 CHARGER II

"The sporty appeal of fastback styling combined with advanced interior innovations" was how Dodge described its latest 'idea' car, when the Charger II was unveiled in 1965. Unlike the first Charger concept, this sleek, ultra-modern car was brand new from the ground up, and owed its appearance to no other vehicle on the highway.

At that time, the 53in high Pale Silver Metallic machine was described as 'remarkably low.' Unlike every other car of that era, it had no visible bumpers. The substantial horizontal chrome bars between the unique headlamps at the front, and the red brake light across the full-width of the rear, gave the Charger II a wide, low, hunkered-down-to-the-road image. The absence of front quarter-lights and B-pillars, plus four fully wind-down windows, created an open-sided feel to the cab,

while unique flush door handles, the absence of applied moldings and distinctive cast magnesium Halibrand wheels, all combined to create a car with real poise. The cabin featured a prominent central console running the entire length of the interior, with individual bucket seats for the driver and three passengers.

The two rear seats could be folded together or separately to create a versatile luggage area big enough to accommodate skis, water skis, fishing and hunting equipment – although there was no liftback to aid access. The seats were trimmed in high-grade, pale silver, long-lasting metallic vinyl backed with super-foam padding and seat belts were provided for all four occupants.

Power came from a mighty 318in^3 (5211cc) V8, punching out 230bhp at 4400rpm and 340lb-ft of torque at just 2400rpm.

The 1965 Dodge Charger II idea car was used to gauge public reaction to a fastback body. Shown at the Chicago Automobile Show, it caused quite a stir. Using the 117in Coronet wheelbase and drivetrain, the Charger indicated how smooth Dodge could be. No protrusions could be seen from any angle. Concealed latches replaced conventional door handles, there were no vent panes because of the three large intakes on the cowl, and used air was discharged through three vents atop each rear fender. No side trim or bumpers appeared, either.

1965 Charger II show car interior. The bucket seats came with built-in vents. Arm rests were on the doors and center console. The console also held the auto-shift and power window controls, and a complete instrument panel sat behind the three-spoke wheel.

1965 Charger II. The huge sweeping rear deck and full-width taillights were prophetic. This concept car would go into production the following year and, for the most part, fairly unchanged. Dodge's 'personal car' elegantly spoke of performance with style, and used the delta theme.

1965 Charger II show car dash. Four space-age large round nacelles held, from left to right, amperage and fuel gauge, speedometer, tachometer and temperature and oil gauges. Performance with style – these gauges would appear on the production model just eighteen months later.

1968 – Daroo I.

THE 1968 DAROO I

Named after the early Anglo-Saxon word for dart or spear, the Daroo 1 show car was unusual in that the bodywork was not done by Ghia or in-house. The famous customizer Barris of California was given a new Dart GT Sport, and along with Chrysler design staff, given the task of making the car look as if it was in motion even when standing still. While retaining the standard wheelbase, the nose was extended by a dramatic 17in, the rear was chopped 10in, and the windshield was lowered to 42 inches. The result was finished in Pearl Honey Yellow with a 'bumble-bee' racing stripe. All the glass had a charcoal smoked tint, which provided an excellent polarizing factor and also protected the cockpit occupants from most ultra-violet rays. The interior was trimmed in matte or semi-gloss textured fabrics to reduce reflections and the twin, height-adjustable, high-back seats sported a new, heavy, coarse-grain vinyl, which moved and stretched to better accommodate the occupants.

Power was supplied by the latest 349in³ (5719cc) 275bhp engine, driving the rear wheels through a four-speed manual shift transmission. The bonnet brandished eight large trumpet intakes, to force-feed air into the single four-barrel carburetor, while each side sill featured a giant exhaust pipe.

THE 1970 YELLOW JACKET

Although a one-off show car, the Dodge Yellow Jacket of 1970 was not so much a way-out concept car, as a sporty evolution of the Challenger – dressed up with a number of 'Scat Pack' features that were available as options on several contemporary Dodge production models. Designed by Dodge engineers and built in Dearborn by Synthetex Inc., the Yellow Jacket was finished in Pearlescent Honey Gold with twin contrasting side stripes that flowed along the belt-line to disappear into the air scoops above the rear wheels.

Preempting today's many 'targa-top' sports car models, the Yellow Jacket had a removable roof panel and integral chrome roll-over bar built into the B-pillars behind the two-seater cockpit. The show car's high-performance image was boosted by four SuperLite headlamps, an

1970 – Yellow Jacket.

air-dam nose spoiler, a 'shaker'-style bonnet top air intake, side air scoops, side-mounted exhaust pipes, deeply dished 15in alloy wheels and a full-width aerodynamic rear wing, which could be raised and lowered electrically via a dashboard switch.

The cockpit accommodated twin high-back bucket seats trimmed in black, nestled into a moulded rear bulkhead painted to match the exterior body color. The sporty open-car feeling could be enhanced by lowering the powered rear window between the B-pillars. Even with the roof on and windows up, a fresh atmosphere could be achieved thanks to the flow-through ventilation system that extracted stale air via vents in the rear deck.

Beneath the sporty exterior, the Yellow Jacket was equipped with a selection of Scat Pack hardware to deliver genuine high-performance, including: a 426in^3 (6980 cc) Hemi engine, manual four-speed transmission, heavy-duty suspension and brakes, and extra-wide Goodyear tires.

THE 1971 DIAMANTE

This was the result of combining two production vehicles, the Challenger and Charger. A sculptured sloping front end added downward air pressure and included aerodynamic retractable headlamps. Side-mounted exhaust pipes and air intakes ventilated and cooled the

1971 – Diamante.

The 1982 Dodge Challenger 'Mr Clean' concept car was based on the Mitsubishi-built Challenger and Plymouth Sapporo coupé. Built to test market reaction in California, Mr Clean had special features that included functional rear deck airfoil, special wheels and tires, a sleek front air-dam, and an aerodynamic 'XG3' front end treatment, giving the look of a larger Dodge Mirada. The car was powered by a silent-shaft 155.9in³ straight-four engine with a five-speed manual transmission.

1987 Intrepid. Dodge concept becomes reality. Built in 1987 and introduced during the 1988 Auto Show season as a 'Dodge of tomorrow', the Intrepid concept car provided design inspiration for the 1991 Dodge Stealth.

426in³ Hemi V8 that via a 4-speed manual transmission, powered the rear wheels. Inside the bright orange colored car, a removable roof panel revealed a built in chrome roll bar. The rear windshield, housed in the flying buttress roof panel, could be electrically lowered from the drivers position. If you think it looks familiar, that's because this car was the Yellow Jacket from 1970 until it was modified and renamed!

THE 1982 CHALLENGER 'MR CLEAN'

This concept was based on the Mitsubishi-built Challenger and Plymouth Sapporo coupé. Built to test market reaction in California, 'Mr Clean' had special features that included functional rear deck airfoil, special wheels and tires, a sleek front air-dam and an

aerodynamic 'XG3' front end treatment, giving the look of a larger Dodge Mirada. The car was powered by a 'silent shaft' 155.9in³ straight-four engine with a five-speed manual transmission.

THE 1987 INTREPID

Also nicknamed the 'Big Shot', the Intrepid was introduced for the 1988 show season as a 'Dodge of tomorrow'. Developed around the Daytona chassis and mechanics, the wedge-shaped body featured aggressive aerodynamics and an aircraft-style bubble canopy. Motion was gained through a 5-speed manual gearbox matched to a mid-engine 2.2-liter Turbo III 4-cylinder power plant, offering 225hp. The bodywork was finished in shades of candy red and orange and featured dual NACA air ducts behind the doors.

THE 1989 VIPER

In the last few years of the eighties and into the nineties, Chrysler produced an amazing selection of concept cars. Some were a lot more viable than others. The 1987 Intrepid and 1990 Daytona R/T, for example, were realistic idea platforms. Others, like the Grand Voyager III, were pure James Bond type vehicles. Unlike most other manufacturers, Chrysler actually started to put some of these dream cars into production and in 1989 the amazing Dodge Viper RT/10 concept car hit the show circuit.

Taking its heritage partly from the Shelby American Cobra Daytona and the Hemi-powered Cunningham coupes of the 1950s, the Viper was conceived as a grand touring car in the traditional sense, following in the footsteps of some of the greatest GTs ever built and taking Dodge sports cars into the next millennium. The concept car expressed how Chrysler felt about the future of performance cars. The future looked fast! Not since the Corvette had there been a true American sports car. The Viper almost single-handedly rekindled the excitement and passion in Mopar power lovers that had lain dormant since the demise of the muscle car in the early seventies.

The idea was simple: to build the quickest, sexiest, most exciting and uncompromising American sports car ever made. A special team was put together at Chrysler's Advanced Styling Studio to design and build this dream

1989 Viper concept. The V10-powered Dodge Viper, the star of the 1989 Auto Show circuit, was given the go-ahead for limited production by Chrysler Chairman Lee Iacocca. At top is the Dodge Viper concept vehicle; an early rendering of the production car is pictured below.

car. On 4 January 1989, the Viper RT/10 made its world debut at the North American International Auto Show in Detroit. Any worries from the concept team about the cars acceptance were soon gone. The public response to the Viper was nothing short of staggering. Orders flooded in, and this was long before the decision to build a production car was taken. The bright red two-door, two-seater open top car was built around a tubular space frame using resin transfer moulded plastic and aluminum panels. As with most ChryCo concepts, the Viper was a fully functional vehicle and the big block V10 power plant augmented the very muscular theme of the car.

THE 1991 NEON

With its happy faced headlights and sub-compact cab-forward design, was created to appeal to a younger market. Debuting at the Detroit Auto Show in January of 1991, the Neon featured electric sliding doors, which opened to reveal a spacious 5-seat interior made possible by the cab forward layout. The seats, stereo and headrest speakers were all easily removable and when the sun shines bright, the fabric roof could be rolled back for convertible style driving. The car was powered by a direct-injection 3-cylinder, 2-stroke 1.1-liter engine that burned alternative fuel that produced over 100hp. With the environment at the forefront of the design, almost 100 per cent of the Neon was recyclable; it even had a garbage compactor built into the trunk! At its inception and through

1991 Neon.

its development to the production vehicle of 1994, many other styles were proposed, including a roadster version and a race car. Some of these never got past the drawing board stage, whilst others were actually built.

THE 1994 VENOM

Sticking to its reptilian theme, 1994 saw the launch of one of Dodge's most exciting concepts, the Venom. The traditional long nose and short deck of the sports car was replaced with a sleek cab-forward design with deeper Viper-esque body sides. Based very loosely on the Neon floor pan, the longer wheelbase and wider track pushed the wheels outwards, allowing agile handling along with a comfortable ride. Painted in a vivid reptilian Venom Yellow Green Pearl, the car was hard to miss and was a glimpse into the future of how smooth a grand tourer sport coupé could look. Power was supplied to the rear wheels by Chrysler's 3.5-liter, 24-valve V6 that gave 245 horsepower.

1994 Venom.

THE 1997 COPPERHEAD

Inspired by the Austin Healey 3000, the 1997 Copperhead was a front engine, rear-wheel-drive, two-seat roadster convertible. While comparisons to the Dodge Viper were inevitable, Copperhead struck its own distinct image with its sleek dimensions. Compared to the Viper, Copperhead measured three inches (76mm) narrower, 8in (203mm) shorter, with an extra 12in (304mm) of wheelbase. Copperhead's interior was designed to complement the serpentine exterior and featured contoured bucket seats with an unconventional Deep Amethyst snakeskin-like leather finish. The tachometer was placed at the centerline of the driver while gauges, HVAC, and radio/cassette controls were smartly placed in the center stack. The center console featured the gearshift and door lock/window controls. When viewed in its entirety, the center console and instrument pod has an uncanny likeness to the

head of a copperhead snake. The car was reported to have 37 coats of Copper Fire Orange paint, which made it shimmer and glow from different angles.

The Copperhead's 135mph top speed was delivered by an all-new, aluminum block, high-output 2.7-liter four cam V6, which churned out 220hp (162kW). The engine was coupled to a close ratio, five-speed manual transmission, sending power to the Copperhead's cast aluminum wheels (18x8in front, 20x9in rear) and tires (complete with snakeskin tread).

At its launch, rumours were rife that it would go into production in the next millennium, but Dodge was concentrating on a new, fast growing market, the sports utility, and although a fantastic looking car, it remained a concept.

THE 1999 CHARGER R/T

Dodge revived the Charger name with this completely restyled body. The Charger R/T had a low, thrusting

1997 Copperhead.

hood and short rear deck and was powered by a super-charged 4.7-liter, 325hp SOHC 16-valve V8 matched to a 5-speed manual transmission, which drove the rear wheels. It was an important car in terms of design, because it showed how Chrysler saw the future of American muscle cars. The interior took styling cues from its 1970s namesake, with retro radio knobs and 3-spoke steering wheel but added modern touches of exposed metal accents and carbon-fiber bucket seats. The Charger ran on compressed natural gas for very low emissions.

The Charger R/T concept car was unveiled during the 1999 auto show season as a platform for Dodge's alternative fuel program. The long, low menacing body with its high rear end owes a lot to its late 1960s namesake, but this is no gas guzzler. The supercharged, 4.7-liter, single overhead cam V8 packs a ferocious 325bhp, but runs from compressed natural gas (CNG).

At the dawn of a new millennium the future looked very good, and it looked like this – the latest concept to come from DaimlerChrysler, the 2001 Dodge Viper GTSR Concept Vehicle. Very similar to the Viper GT2 limited edition, the 2001 GTSR was a street-legal, Le Mans endurance race-inspired concept which, in the words of Chrysler's chief designer Tom Gale, "shows the potential we have".

THE 2000 VIPER GTSR

This Viper concept was almost completely new from the ground up. This coupé sat 2in lower to the ground and 3½in lower overall than the production GTS from 2000. It used the same 488in³ aluminum V10 but with an added 50hp, bringing it up to 500 horses. The concept also kept the space frame and aluminum suspension, but the one-piece carbon fiber body was dramatically different. With a longer wheelbase and wider track, the GTSR looked more muscular than any Viper before. The rear wheels were pushed back 3in and the A-pillar brought forward 3in to allow for a larger door. At the front, a lower hood incorporated a larger grille opening, integrated louvers and a larger NACA air-intake duct. An electronically adjustable front wind-splitter, large rear air diffuser and huge cockpit- controlled rear spoiler all helped to keep the car on the ground while it accelerated to 60mph in 3.75 seconds and its estimated top speed of over 200mph. Aimed at the public as a tourer, the interior featured all the bells and whistles, including a high spec stereo, air-con, adjustable pedals and lots of billet aluminum accents.

THE 2001 NEON SRT

The year 2000 saw the launch of Dodge's restyled Neon compact and to add to the excitement, Chrysler's team at Performance Vehicle Operations (PVO) department came up with arguably the fastest compact in America. This 'Neon on steroids' was the most powerful Neon ever, with a supercharged, 2.0-liter, 16-valve engine that generated more than 200hp. It showed how much potential Neon had in what has become a huge market – the customization of compact cars.

The craze emerged in the mid 1990s in Southern California, and gradually spread across the states. Japanese imports were the main focus of the sport compact 'tuners'. But as the craze spread, tuners looked for something different from the boxy Hondas and Toyotas, so more domestic cars were being slammed and tweaked. In answer to this, the Neon SRT concept was intended to stimulate the imagination of 18 to 25 year-old drivers as to what they could do with the right accessories if they owned a Neon.

The Neon SRT had a boldly styled front fascia, projector-beam fog lamps, a hood air scoop and an

2001 Neon SRT.

imposing rear spoiler. Its 2.0-liter, SOHC, 4-cylinder engine had 208 horsepower and 180lb-ft of torque, which allowed for a 0 to 60 time of just 5.9 seconds and a top speed of 148mph. By comparison, the production Neon had 132 horsepower. In addition, SRT sat 1.5in lower than the production Neon. It had 4-wheel independent suspension with Eibach custom springs, Tokico performance-tuned struts, heavy-duty front and rear sway bars, racing tires and 17in aluminum alloy wheels.

A sound system sounding more like a concert hall than a compact car was made up of an Alpine in-dash compact disc changer/cassette/receiver/sound field processor, operated through Precision Power 400 and Precision 1800 amplifiers and four JBL two-way speakers. The system was rounded off with two Infinity 12in subwoofers. In 2003 Dodge launched an even more powerful concept, the SRT4, followed quickly by the SRT4 Extreme. These cars were used as platforms for performance bolt-on accessories for the same 18 to 25 year-old 'tuner' market. Positive reaction to these cars brought forth the production model of the SRT4.

THE 2003 DODGE RAZOR

The Razor concept car was a joint effort between the Chrysler Group

design studios in Auburn Hills, Michigan and Carlsbad, California, and Razor USA, the kick-scooter manufacturer. Inspired by classic European sports cars of the 1960s, a modern minimalist design philosophy was utilized. Searching

for a name that reflected the car's energy and attitude, the Chrysler Group approached Razor USA to form a licensing partnership with the trendsetting and youthful Razor brand. To keep costs down the corporate parts bin was raided, which offered many suspension and underbody components. While the six-speed manual transmission was developed in Stuttgart, Germany, the engine was an upgraded version of Chrysler's 2.4-liter inline DOHC 4-cylinder, now with a turbocharger and intercooler. The engine developed 187kW (250bhp) and 312Nm (230lb-ft) of torque. Aimed at young driving enthusiasts, the Razor concept was designed with a targeted sticker price of $14,500 within the USA. The Dodge Razor's instrument cluster had an integrated tachometer/speedometer with analogue reading

2003 Dodge Razor.

2001 Super8 Hemi concept car was a great mix of retro styling, encompassing the best from car and truck design, wrapped in a modern package. The tall stance of this concept showed the way Dodge's production cars would go in the near future, and that low, 1950s wrap-around front screen was sublime, matching the rock 'n' roll dash and instrument cluster inside. The bold, in-your-face powerful stance left admirers in no doubt that this vehicle could perform. Fitted with a prototype 353in^3 (5.7-liter) pushrod V8 engine featuring hemispherical combustion chambers and two sparkplugs per cylinder, the Super8 Hemi offered 353 horsepower (263 kW) and 395 lb-ft (536 Nm) of torque. When delivered to the rear wheels via a four-speed AutoStick manumatic transmission, it allowed the vehicle to reach 60mph (97kph) in less than six seconds, and clock a top speed of 154mph (248 kph). Wow!

of the revs and a digital read-out of the speed. The interior was finished in body color and extruded aluminum. The package also included two orange Razor scooters in the trunk.

THE 2003 MAGNUM SRT

It had been more than 30 years since Dodge ruled the streets with Hemi power and rear-wheel-drive performance, and when Dodge released its latest concept on the 2nd January 2003, it threw away the rule book. Dodge unleashed power in all-new proportions with the introduction of its Dodge Magnum concept. Based on the same LX platform used for the 300C sedan, the Magnum was the station wagon version of that layout, but when you add a Hemi engine topped with a Whipple supercharger, plus unique body styling, you get one very fast and versatile tourer. The legendary engine that powered Dodge's muscle cars of the 1960s had been re-engineered and reborn as a modern, high-performance, fuel-efficient and durable power plant known as the all-new 5.7-liter HEMI V8, and this version offered 430hp.

The Magnum was nothing less than sensational. The long, tapered roof line with minimal front and rear overhang complemented the long powerful hood. The rear cargo door hinged between the C and D-pillars to create a cavernous opening for its large luggage bay. Not since the beautiful Chrysler Town & Country station wagons of the late 1940s had such class emanated from a utility vehicle. Almost simultaneously to its launch in California, Dodge announced a production version would go on sale in 2004, virtually unchanged from the concept vehicle.

THE 2003 AVENGER

Designed to bring together the style and performance of European-type rally cars, with the capability and convenience of American SUVs, the Dodge Avenger concept vehicle made its world debut at the NAIAS in Detroit in early 2003.

2003 Avenger.

The Adrenaline Red Pearl-colored Avenger, with its king-sized 20in diameter alloy wheels and muscular protruding wheel flares, was the complete embodiment of tough, rally car durability plus "high-tech athleticism". Its wide track, deep fenders, ribbed roof and fastback tail displayed the Avenger's all-wheel-drive agility.

Despite its coupé profile, the Avenger had four doors to comply with the 'do more' philosophy of the Dodge brand, and the rear doors opened 90 degrees for the best possible access. The detailing of the Dodge Avenger concept echoed a boldness that resonated with the overall design theme of capability, functionality and stability. The interior was styled with rally car simplicity and a cockpit-like environment punctuated with silver and black detailed accents. The cabin featured four individual seats, fitted with four-point safety harnesses.

In keeping with its exterior image, the Avenger had an all-wheel-drive power train matched to a 3.5-liter V6 engine and an A604 automatic transmission, offering drivers the choice of manual selection, using steering wheel-mounted paddles (first pioneered in rallying) for smooth, quick, direct gear changes and maximum driver involvement. The Avenger would be the car that provided the inspiration for the C-Segment vehicles, spearheading the expansion of the Dodge brand to markets outside North America with cars like the Caliber.

THE 2003 DODGE TOMAHAWK

Dodge revealed many concepts this year including the Kahuna and others mentioned already, but the strangest must be this next one. Not a car by any stretch of the imagination, and one of Chrysler's nuttiest concepts, but its power alone makes it worthy of a mention here. The Viper-powered Dodge Tomahawk concept shattered all the barriers of conventional thinking about personal transportation, when it roared into public view at the 2003 North American International Auto Show. It was a creation that utterly redefined the term 'super bike'. The Tomahawk was a rolling sculpture, combining art deco styling with extreme automotive thinking. It was extreme engineering

2003 Tomahawk.

that led to the birth of this four-wheel 'bike,' created around and showcasing the awesome 505in³, 8.3-liter aluminum Viper V10 engine. Five hundred horsepower and 525lb-ft of torque transmitted through the dual rear wheels gave this radical vehicle a theoretical top speed of 420mph – for anyone crazy enough to try it. It moved the idea of design concept vehicles to a completely new level, and as the Chrysler Group's Head of Design, Trevor Creed, told the audience when the Tomahawk roared onto the Press conference stage in Detroit, "Grab life by the horns… and hang on!"

Dodge built several more Tomahawks as non-operational sculptures that were available through the Neiman Marcus catalogue for a bargain $555,000 price tag!

THE 2004 SLING SHOT

Another year and another concept, and for 2004 it was the Sling Shot. Introduced in January of that year, the Sling Shot was designed as an affordable, entry-level sports car for those with a penchant for fresh air. The Sling Shot featured a main roof panel and side rails over the passenger area that could be stored in the trunk, while a canvas roof panel slid back and out of the way like a rolltop desk for open-air driving.

In times of rising gas prices, one of the Sling Shot's main aims was frugality, and even though its rear-mounted, 3-cylinder, petrol engine delivered 100bhp and a 0-60mph time of about 10 seconds, due to a power to weight ratio of 17.4lb/bhp it got up to 45mpg. A five-speed gearbox, rack-and-pinion steering, four-wheel independent suspension and four-wheel disc brakes completed the driver-oriented power train.

THE 2006 CHALLENGER

On 8 January 2006, the latest creation from Chrysler Group's West Coast Pacifica Studio charged onto the international stage when the Dodge Challenger concept was unleashed. Not by chance did it look like the original Challenger from the seventies. When in its design phase, they brought into the studio a 1970 Challenger as inspiration. A hard act to follow, some would say.

Based on Chrysler's latest LX platform, the rear-wheel driven, Hemi-powered performance coupé evokes sweet memories of the earlier classic Mopar muscle car, but with a unique contemporary look all its own. With a wheelbase 6in longer and a track 2in wider than the original, the 2006 Challenger looks even tougher and more purposeful than the '70s version. With front and rear tracks at 64 and 65in respectively, the Challenger is wider than any other LX car before it. The signature coke-bottle belt line is higher on the body, kicking up just before the rear wheelarch. The five-spoke chrome wheels, 20in front and 21in rear, are set flush with the body side, helping to give the car that muscular stance.

The distinctive 'performance hood' and its twin diagonal scoops, now with functional butterfly-valve intakes, is the most obvious design cue taken from the original. However, to showcase the modern techniques

The 2004 Sling Shot.

2006 Challenger.

used in fabricating the car, what look like painted racing stripes are actually the exposed carbon fiber of the hood material. Inside the car, more homage is paid to the first Challenger – with its thick, easy-grip rim, circular hub and pierced silver spokes, the leather-wrapped steering wheel evokes the original car's 'Tuff' wheel, as does the steering column 'ribbing'. The floor console, its center surface tipped toward the driver, is fitted with a proper 'pistol grip' shifter shaped to master the quick, crisp shifts possible with the six-speed manual gearbox. Finished in Orange Pearl, the car is a genuine two-door hardtop with no B-pillar, but still comfortably seats four. Will it go into production? Dodge currently has no 2-doors in its range and no coupes, so it was no surprise when Chrysler's CEO announced in July 2006 that it would enter production for the 2008 model year. But if Dodge really want to pay homage to the 70s classic, how about building a convertible Challenger? Now that would be something else!

THE 2006 HORNET

Revealed at the 2006 Geneva Motor Show, the Hornet is a strong contender for the ugliest Dodge ever built. A tall, wide box on wheels sums up the little design effort that went into this vehicle. In its favor, it does have a supercharged 170hp 1.6-liter OHC 4-cylinder engine, which will take it to 60mph in 6.7 seconds and gives a top speed of 130mph, and with those huge 19in wheels positioned as far into the corners as possible, it should be quite stable ... but would you want to be seen in this? Dodge is threatening to build this for the European market along with the Jeep-based Nitro. It is incredible to think that the same division of Chrysler can come out with two such totally different concepts within weeks of each other. The strikingly beautiful Challenger and this thing!

2006 Hornet.

2007 Avenger R/T concept. The very latest concept from Dodge went into production for Europe and North America in the winter of 2006, virtually unchanged. The tough looking Avenger will be sold as a 2008 within the usually sober D-segment of the world market, and offers something refreshingly different from standard sedans; a mid-size car that is bold, powerful, capable and street smart. The chiselled features hark back to the golden age of Mopar Muscle. Its side profile is distinguished by a long hood and short deck lid proportions, with muscular rear shoulders and a sleek rear spoiler. This concept's long greenhouse is created by the use of a high-gloss black B-pillar, and aerodynamically-inspired rear door appliques, which make this mid-size sedan look like it's pouncing forward even when at a standstill. The concept is powered by a 2.0-liter turbo diesel, which will be available on the production model, along with a selection of petrol engine and performance options.

It would be impossible to list the specifications for all of the performance cars listed in this book, so I have selected a few of the production cars that I feel were milestone vehicles, to give you a chance to compare them and see how they evolved.

1956 D-500

Body types:	2-door hardtop, 2-door coupé or convertible
Engine:	315in³ V8, cast iron block, hemispherical combustion chambers, overhead valves
Bore and stroke:	3.63X3.80
Compression ratio:	9.25:1
Bhp:	260@4400rpm
Transmission:	3-speed column-mounted manual gearbox, Powerflite 2-speed automatic optional extra
Chassis features:	Wheelbase 120in, overall length 212in, heavy-duty double-channelled box section chassis
Brakes:	Heavy-duty Imperial 12in drum brakes all round
Weight:	2-door hardtop 3505lb, convertible 3630lb
Production:	Not available for D-500

1966 CHARGER

Body types:	2-door fastback
Engine:	318in³ V8, cast iron block, overhead valve
Bore and stroke:	3.91x3.31
Compression ratio:	9.0:1
Bhp:	230@4400rpm
Optional engines:	361in³ V8 (265bhp), 426in³ Hemi V8 (425bhp)
Transmission:	3-speed manual or 3-speed Torqueflite automatic (both floor mounted), 4-speed manual optional extra
Chassis features:	Wheelbase 117in, overall length 203.6in, standard Coronet chassis
Suspension:	Front torsion bar suspension, solid rear axle with semi-elliptical leaf springs
Brakes:	Total contact drum brakes all round
Weight:	3499lb
Production:	37,344

1968 CORONET R/T

Body types:	2-door hardtop or convertible
Engine:	440in³ V8, cast iron block, wedge cylinder head
Bore and stroke:	4.32x3.75
Compression ratio:	10.0:1
Bhp:	375@4400rpm
Optional engines:	426in³ Hemi V8 (425bhp)
Transmission:	Torqueflite 3-speed automatic with floor mounted shifter
Chassis features:	Wheelbase 117in, overall length 207in, standard chassis with firm-ride shock absorbers
Suspension:	Rallye suspension
Brakes:	Heavy-duty drum brakes
Weight:	3353lb (hardtop coupé), 3613lb (convertible)
Production:	10,849

1969 CHARGER DAYTONA

Body types:	2-door semi-fastback with 23in high rear wing and 18in nose cone
Engine:	440in³ Magnum V8, details as above
Optional engines:	426in³ Hemi V8 (425bhp)
Transmission:	Four-speed manual transmission with Hurst floor shift
Chassis features:	Wheelbase 117in, overall length 225.9in, heavy-duty chassis
Suspension:	Front torsion bar suspension, solid rear axle with leaf springs
Brakes:	HD drum brakes
Weight:	3700lb
Production:	505 (official figure)

1984 (OMNI) SHELBY CHARGER

Body types:	2-door hatchback coupé
Engine:	135in³ (2.2-liter) cast iron block, aluminum head, overhead cam straight four
Bore and stroke:	3.44x3.62
Compression ratio:	9.6:1
Bhp:	110@5600rpm
Transmission:	4-speed manual standard, Torqueflite automatic and 5 speed manual optional extras
Chassis features:	Wheelbase 96.6in, overall length 174.8in
Suspension:	MacPherson Iso-Strut front with coil springs and linkless anti-sway bar, rear leaf springs
Brakes:	Front discs, rear drums
Weight:	2350lb
Production:	7552

1992 VIPER RT/10

Body types:	2-door open roadster
Engine:	488in³ (8.0-liter) aluminum overhead valve V10
Bore and stroke:	4.00x3.88
Compression ratio:	9.6:1
Bhp:	400 (net)
Transmission:	6-speed manual
Chassis features:	Fiberglass and aluminum body on tubular steel space frame, wheelbase 96.2in, overall length 175.1in
Suspension:	Upper and lower 'A' arms, Koni coil springs and shock absorbers and anti-sway bar front and rear
Brakes:	Disc brakes all round
Weight:	3500lb
Production:	162

2005/06 MAGNUM R/T

Body types:	4-door sport tourer
Engine:	345in³ (5.7-liter) 16-valve Hemi V8, aluminum heads on deep skirt cast iron block
Bore and stroke:	3.92x3.58
Compression ratio:	9.6:1
Bhp:	340hp@5000rpm
Transmission:	5-speed automatic with adaptive electronic control or Autostick driver interactive manual control and electronically modulated torque converter
Chassis features:	Unitised steel body, rear-wheel-drive (AWD optional), wheelbase 120.0in, overall length 197.7in

Suspension:	Front – independent SAL with high upper 'A' arm, coil spring over gas-charged shock absorber and stabiliser bar, rear – five-link independent with coil spring and link type stabiliser,
Brakes:	Vented disc brakes all-round with anti-lock and traction control
Weight:	4179lb
Production:	39,795 (total Magnum production, including R/T)

DODGE CHRONOLOGY

1899 Dodge brothers move to Canada and begin building Evans & Dodge bicycle.

1901 The brothers return to Michigan and set up their own automotive parts company.

1902 First Ford motor cars are produced with Dodge-designed and built parts.

1910 New Dodge plant is built at Hamtramck, Detroit, Michigan.

1914 Dodge Brothers Inc created. First Dodge Bros automobile rolls off the production line at Hamtramck.

1915 First year production figure of 45,000 sets a new record.

1920 Both John and Horace die of influenza.

1925 Dillon, Read & Co buys Dodge Bros for $146m – the largest cash transaction thus far in US history.

1925 Walter Percy Chrysler buys Dodge Bros. Dodge introduces its first 6-cylinder engine.

1929 Dodge drop the famous 4-cylinder engine from car production.

1930 Dodge Division introduces its first 8-cylinder engine, a 220.7in^3 straight-eight.

1935 The division builds its 3 millionth car, a four-door touring sedan.

1938 The last year that the intertwined triangle 'Dodge Brothers' badge was used.

1940 Dodge becomes involved with defence prototype vehicles.

1942 Civilian car production ceases for the war effort Dodge build over ½ million vehicles during the war.

1946 As post-war auto production begins, Dodge offers warmed-over 1942 models for the next three years. Red-Ram ornament first seen on Dodge hoods.

1948 Dodge open a new plant in San Leandro, California.

1949 Introduction of the first all-new' post-war Dodge. Chrysler hires stylist Virgil Exner Snr.

1950 Along with other Chrysler divisions, Dodge offers its first pillarless hardtop coupés. Dodge Coronet convertible chosen as official pace car for the Michigan State Fair's 100 mile championship race. Hell Drivers stunt team uses a Wayfarer in its 'flaming jump' routine.

1951 Introduction of the Chrysler 331in^3 Firepower Hemi V8 engine. Dodge offers 'tip-toe' semi-automatic gearchange. Korean war effort means 1951 and 1952 models are almost identical.

1952 Hemi-powered cars compete in NASCAR and at Le Mans with promising results.

1953 All-new styling includes Jet-Flow air scoop hood. Introduction of the 241.3in^3 Red Ram Hemi engine. Dodge V8 wins Mobile Economy Run. New speed record of 102.6mph set at El Mirage dry lake. Lee Petty captures Dodge's first Grand National win.

1954 The first modest fins seen on a production Dodge. Dodge paces Indy 500 race. Dodge sets 196 AAA stock car records at Bonneville, Utah. Dodge sweeps the Mexican Road Race taking the top four positions. Powerflite fully automatic transmission is introduced. Dodge's first ever concept car – the Firearrow – debuts.

1955 The first-generation Forward Look, tri-tone paint schemes and polyspherical head engine introduced. Dodge offers a car for the ladies – the La Femme. Dodge Hemi grows to 270.1in^3, offering 193bhp.

1956 Dodge releases its first performance model – the D-500. 12 volt electrical system made standard. Super Red Ram debuts.

1957 Second generation Forward Look styling, torsion bar suspension and Torqueflite three-speed automatic transmission introduced. D-500 is relegated to an options package.

1958 Don 'Big Daddy' Garlits breaks the 170mph barrier in his 'Swamp Rat' Hemi dragster. Hemi V8 is dropped for the new wedge-head Ram Fire motor. Quad headlights become standard.

1959 Dodge finally drops the L-head Six engine. All Dodge cars receive a heavy face-lift, and swivel seats are available as an option along with a host of other gadgets.The most powerful Dodge engine yet, the 345bhp Super D-500, is optional on all cars.

1960 Smaller Dart models, new slant-six and uni-body construction introduced. A Dart Phoenix sets a new world record of 191.8mph at the Bonneville

Speed Trials. The D-500 383in³ V8 could be fitted with a ram-induction manifold.

1961 The Valiant-based Lancer 170 and 770 are released, with a smooth 225in³ slant six. Racers can order a Hyper-Pak to boost power to over 275hp. Full-size models can opt for a 413in³ V8, which offers up to 375bhp.

1962 Dodge introduces the 410bhp 413in³ Ramcharger Max-Wedge engine. A host of after-sales Mopar high-performance parts are available to hot-rodders, including manifolds, headers and cams. Down-sizing cars is the latest Detroit craze.

1963 An improved Ramcharger debuted in the form of the 426-A, giving 425bhp. The Ramchargers drag team wins the NHRA Nationals Super Stock finals.

1964 Dodge celebrates its fiftieth anniversary. The factory builds a limited number of lightweight, altered wheel-base drag cars. At the drag strip, Dodge drivers use the new 426in³ Race-Hemi to clean up. Ramcharger's Jim Thornton wins the US Nationals in his auto-gearbox "Candymatic" Dodge. Joe Public can order a tamer 426 Street Wedge.

1965 Bob Summers sets present 409.227mph Land Speed Record in "Goldenrod" using four Hemis in tandem. Ex-Chrysler chairman K T Keller dies. On the auto-show circuit the predictive Dodge Charger II shows what next years fastback will look like.

1966 Chrysler builds the "Street Hemi" and returns to NASCAR racing. The Coronet-based Charger fastback is released as a production car. Dodge Charger wins the NASCAR Championship, Plymouth is second.

1967 Don White's Charger gives Hemi-powered cars second USAC championship in a row. A Coronet R/T (Road & Track) is for sale with a 440in³ Magnum V8 as standard.

1968 Dodge produces a limited number of 426in³ Super Stock Darts. A bare bones SuperBee coupé is added to the Coronet line-up.

1969 Dodge introduces Charger 500 HEM, which wins 22 NASCAR races. Dodge builds over 500 Charger Daytonas. The 'winged' 1969 Dodge Charger Daytona with Hemi power reigns over NASCAR super speedways.

1970 Buddy Baker is the first to break 200mph on a closed course in a Hemi Dodge Charger Daytona stock car. Bobby Isaac sets a closed course speed record – 201.104 mph – in a Dodge Charger Daytona after winning the NASCAR championship. Late into the 'pony car' market, the new Challenger goes up against the Mustang, Camaro and Cougar.

1971 Bobby Isaac breaks 28 records at Bonneville in a Dodge Charger Daytona – top speed is 217.368mph. Last year for the true R/T nameplate and Dodge convertibles, until their revival in the eighties. The short-lived Dart Demon name is introduced mid-year, but is renamed 'Sport' after complaints are made.

1972 Dodge starts to withdraw its HiPo cars and options, including the Hemi.

1973 OPEC imposes oil embargo, petrol prices rise dramatically and lead to severe fuel shortages.

1974 As the fuel crises fires the final lethal shot in the muscle car wars, Challenger sees its last year of production in a dwindling pony car market.

1976 Dodge releases the compact Aspen as the final Dusters and Darts are built.

1977 Aspen buyers could order R/T and Super Pak optional packages, separately or together.

1981 The K-cars arrive to much acclaim.

1983 A new Omni-based Shelby Charger goes on sale with a 2.2-liter in-line four.

1984 The die-hard slant-six engine sees its final year of production in passenger cars.

1989 Viper concept car released to overwhelming support. Public pressure for a production Viper.

1990 Intrepid concept shows the way forward.

1992 Viper R/T10 hits the road. Dodge releases a limited number of Daytona IROC R/Ts.

1993 Chrysler bring in its Cab-forward styling to the Dodge Intrepid.

1995 New Stratus and Avenger hit the showrooms.

1996 Dodge paces the Indy 500 with the new Viper GTS coupé.

1998 Neon R/T coupé is available with an ACR race package. Viper wins at Le Mans. Charger concept debuts.

1999 Dodge announces return to NASCAR. Viper gets an ACR package, wins in the FIA GT2 series and at Le Mans.

2001 Dodge Intrepid returns to NASCAR at the Daytona 500.

2002 Intrepid wins at the Daytona 500.

2003 New 5.7-liter Hemi Magnum develops up to 345hp and 375lb-ft of torque. Fastest Viper ever – the competition coupé – goes on sale to 'racers only'. Production of the SRT4 starts in the spring of 2003 at Belvidere, Illinois.

2004 The first Dodge production car in over 33 years powered by a Hemi engine goes on sale, the Magnum.

2005 Charger race car unveiled to coincide with launch of new production Charger. Latest Viper, the SRT10 coupé revealed.

2006 Dodge launches in Europe and UK with Caliber and Nitro.

2007 Dodge releases the limited edition Charger SRT8 SuperBee.

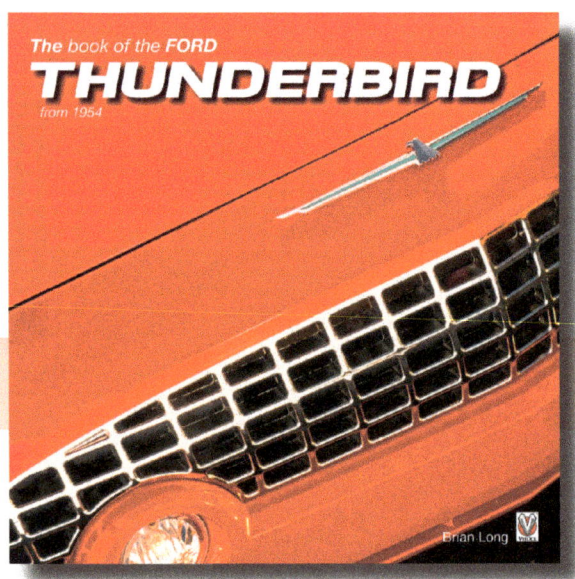

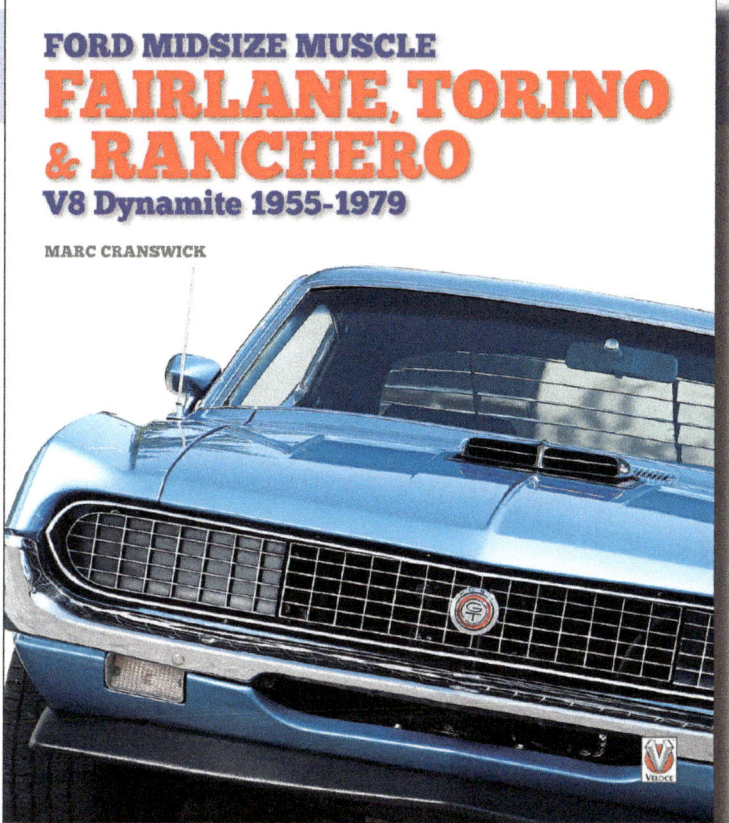

FORD MIDSIZE MUSCLE: FAIRLANE, TORINO & RANCHERO

- ISBN: 978-1-845849-29-0
- Hardback
- 176 pages
- 229 pictures

This book details the evolution of Ford's family car through the golden era of Detroit. It tells how Henry Ford took the no-frills Fairlane, added more zing to create the Torino, and satisfied America's luxury desires with the LTD II; and follows the evolution of Ford's midsize muscle cars, to the creation of the first car-based pickup – the Ranchero.

FORD GT THEN, AND NOW

- ISBN: 978-1-787111-26-4
- Hardback
- 240 pages
- 491 colour and b&w photos

Starting in 1956 when Ford officially entered motor racing, this book takes the reader on a journey through the history of the GT, and introduces the personalities behind all the different Ford GT development programs, old and new.

For more details visit www.veloce.co.uk • email info@veloce.co.uk • tel 0(44) 01305 260068

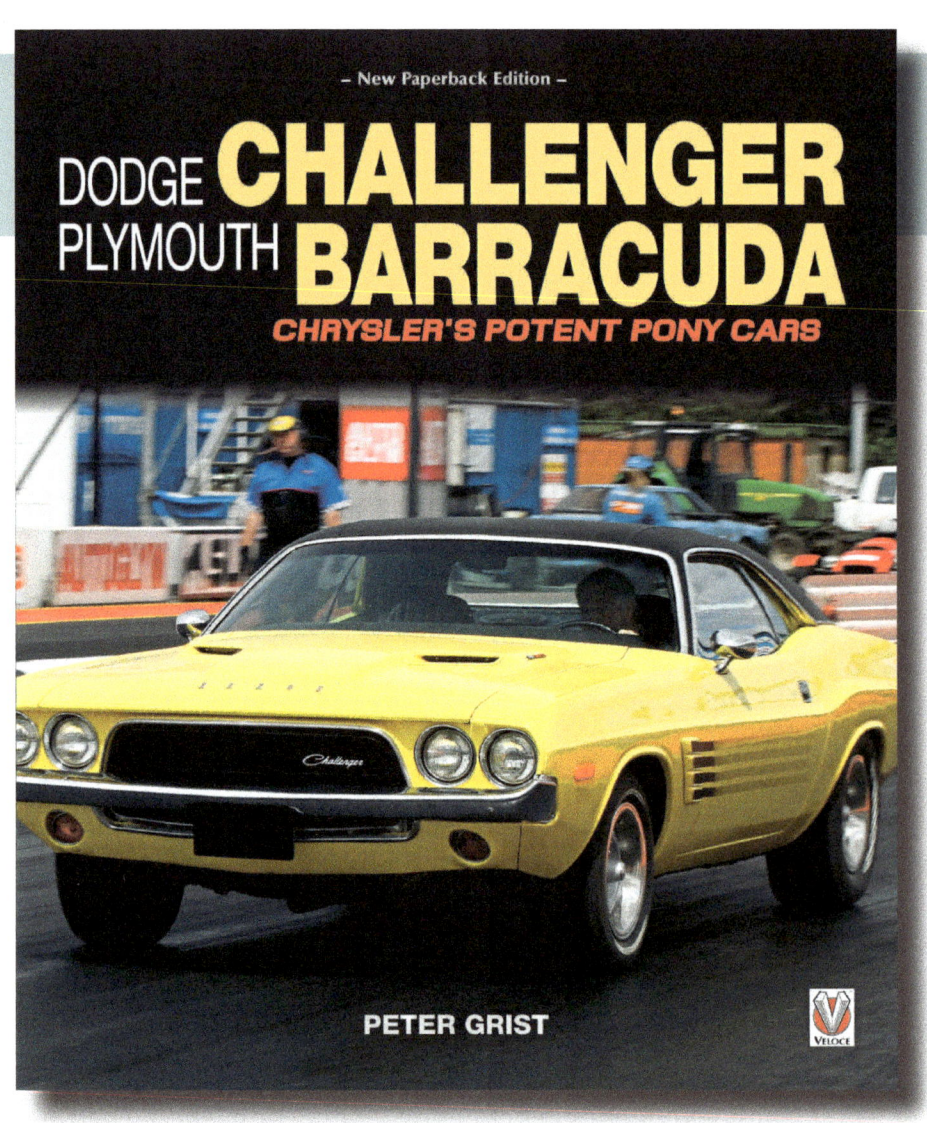